FOOD ADDICTS

FOOD ADDICTS

Top 10 Tips to Stop Compulsive Overeating

Felicity Garver

Benesserra
Publishing

Los Angeles, California

Benesserra Publishing
1827 Barry Ave.
Los Angeles, CA 90025

First Edition
Paperback: ISBN: 978-0-9884917-5-5

Printed in the United States of America on acid-free paper.

DISCLAIMER

Nothing contained in this book is intended to constitute, nor should it be considered as, medical advice or to serve as a substitute for the advise of a physician or other qualified health care provider. We make no assurances of the information being suited to your medical needs, and disclaim any implications that the content of this book is suitable for every person.

This program and its contents should not be construed as professional medical service or advice, do not constitute a doctor/patient or therapist/patient relationship and are not intended to diagnose, treat, cure, or take the place of any such advice or care.

Felicity Garver and Benesserra Publishing provide this content for entertainment and informational purposes only. The program and its advice do not constitute, and should not be interpreted as medical advice or opinion. Felicity Garver is not a medical professional and does not provide medical services or render medical advice. The program and author's suggestions are not a substitute for the advice of a medical professional, and any advice contained herein should not be relied upon to make medical decisions, to diagnose or treat any medical or health condition.

If you have any health condition requiring medical advice or services, you must consult a medical professional and receive clearance and/or approval from your physician prior to embarking on any kind of exercise or nutritional program. The reader should use caution when embarking on any type of weight loss program, and avoid going to extremes that could put their health at risk.

CONTENTS

INTRODUCTION   1

1 GIVE UP DIETING FOREVER   7

2 MAKE IT OKAY TO EAT ANY KIND OF FOOD   17

3 RELEARN HOW TO EAT   21

4 KNOWING WHAT FOODS YOU WANT AND NEED   36

5 HOW EMOTIONS MASQUERADE AS HUNGER   42

6 EAT WHEN YOU'RE HUNGRY, STOP WHEN YOU'RE FULL   48

7 LEARN POSITIVE SELF TALK, DIET FROM NEGATIVITY   57

8 HOW YOUR EXCESS WEIGHT SERVES YOU   74

9 GET RID OF EMOTIONAL BAGGAGE   89

10 PUTTING THE TIPS INTO PLAY   108

INTRODUCTION

For much of my life, I felt that I had to be thin to be perfect. The problem was that I could never be thin enough to finally understand that I was perfect. I tried all the usual ways to get thin: diets, exercise, fasting, diet pills. And for a while, they worked. But even though I was thin, I never felt good about myself, always thinking I had to be better in some way, in order to be "good enough." I liked myself, but I didn't love myself and I never felt really good about who I was. There was always a nagging feeling that I needed to improve in some way to finally feel good about myself. But I just hadn't found the answer.

Eventually I could not continue with my dieting regimen, as it was making my life unmanageable in many ways. I stopped taking pills and dieting, and my weight ballooned up about thirty pounds. I was horrified. All my ways of coping with my body, food and eating weren't working any more, and I realized that I had been a compulsive eater for a long time. That is, I used food to try to solve problems in my life. When I was frustrated or angry, I used food to soothe or distract myself. This became apparent to me once when I remember standing in front of the open refrigerator thinking, "What am I looking for? There's nothing in here that will help me feel better. In fact, whatever I eat right now will probably make me feel worse." And I not only used food to solve emotional issues, I feared food as well, thinking it had power over me to make me feel bad about myself. I know now that food itself was never the problem. The problem was my relationship to my body and eating.

So I began to understand the dynamics of how my emotions were affecting my behavior around food. I tried various non-diet approaches to achieve my ideal body, and they worked to some extent in healing my relationship with my body. But not until I began to use Vivation, as a technique to resolve negativity, was I able to begin to fully love and accept myself as I am. Using Vivation, combined with other tools for gaining sensitivity to how much food I need to eat, allowed me to reach and maintain my ideal weight. I learned how to deal with my emotions in a way that would go directly to the heart of what was eating at me. I became assertive enough to no longer tolerate the intolerable and became unwilling to stuff my emotions down with food.

Today, I no longer diet, and eat what I want. I no longer criticize myself for my food choices, or believe that any food is bad for me. I no longer relate to any food as forbidden. I can say, "I know I can have it, but do I really WANT it?" regarding any food. I've come to love and feel good about my body, and myself relating to it as a dear friend who has been with me through thick and thin, heavy and light, and as a miraculous instrument through which I experience life.

I feel good about who I am as a person, with all my human foibles and unique strengths. I am much more forgiving of others, and myself and motivate myself positively through enthusiasm and a sense of adventure, rather than thinking myself wrong.

I know you will understand if I say, FOOD IS NOT THE PROBLEM. It's not! Food is healthful and delicious and is meant to be enjoyed. But do you eat food or do you use it? If you use food for any other reason than to fuel your body and satisfy hunger, then you are using food for things that it is not meant to solve. But still, food is not the issue; the problems are your inability to deal with life's stresses and your negative emotions.

The goals of this book are to help you feel comfortable around food, eat when you're hungry and stop when you're full; to teach you to enjoy food without guilt or self-recrimination; to develop the motivation to create your ideal body, and experience increased happiness, satisfaction, well-being and creativity in all areas of your life.

The first and most important goal is to allow you to end dieting forever, because in the long run, diets don't work for weight loss. You will learn to be able to eat what you like, as long as you're following the eating guidelines, and you'll lose weight. You will completely change your relationship to food and eating. You will learn to view food as something pleasurable that you eat when you are hungry to fuel your body, and avoid using food as an all-purpose solution for everything from loneliness to boredom. You will be able to eat anything that you love and enjoy, in the right amounts for you, without feeling guilty or ashamed. By learning how to feed yourself in ways that are self-loving and nurturing, you will stop eating more food than you require. You will lose weight, and reach and maintain your ideal weight without dieting or deprivation.

As an added benefit, when you begin to experience freedom from overeating and compulsive behavior, you will begin to discover how much more creative energy you have for constructive projects.

You will learn to admire and respect yourself for your own uniqueness and abilities and feel better about yourself, exactly the way you are right now. You will find that loving yourself as you are now assists in motivating you positively and paves the way for lasting changes.

Many dieters think that if they stop dieting and eat what they want, their body will sabotage them and grow wildly out of control. As a result, they fear food and eating, and feel that their body is an adversary. Putting these tips into action, you will learn to be in harmony with your body instead of relating to your body as a part of you that needs to be controlled and restrained. You will learn to become your own best friend, cheerleader and self-support system.

Are you using food to deal with life's problems?

We all develop ways of coping with the challenges in our lives. If you eat to soothe or stimulate yourself, or if you feel you can't do something until you are the perfect weight, you are using food to deal with the issues in life, which could be better solved another way. Suppressing your feelings by eating or distracting yourself by beating yourself up takes you farther away from the solution. Although compulsive behavior with food is not as damaging as using other substances, food, dieting, and being obsessed about your body and weight creates havoc in your life. Suppressing your feelings with food is probably one of the least effective and most damaging ways of coping with problems. Quite often, even though we know we are eating for emotional reasons, we simply don't have the tools or methods to deal with our emotion any other way. As you read this, you will start to find other ways to deal with the uncomfortable and troubling emotions that are often the cause of food addiction, compulsive eating and bingeing. By learning to be gentle with yourself and recognizing that your behavior is a protective mechanism, you can begin to expand your awareness of the problem and open the doorway to the solution.

Finally, you will learn about the Vivation technique and be able to practice it with the Vivation CD. Vivation is a powerful self-improvement process for resolving negativity about your emotions and dealing with food cravings. Many people have experience with methods that suggest "feeling your feelings" as a means of recovering from negative or unwanted behavior. The quandary of this however, is that we don't know how to resolve the negativity of those feelings, and consequently are using food to AVOID feeling them. What Vivation can do is begin to heal those emotions at a very deep level, so you no longer are being driven to act in ways that don't serve you, or confound your best intentions to achieve your goals.

Vivation will greatly improve your sense of wellbeing and permanently increase your self-esteem. It will be used as a tool, along with all the other tools you will be learning, to heal negativity and allow you to continually improve your life.

Something appealed to you about the idea of eliminating your addiction to food, because you are reading this. Deep within, your heart resonates with the idea of achieving your ideal body using positive motivation, and loving yourself more. I know you will gain that from this information. This method is magical, because of the deep inner changes that result from your willingness to engage in the healing exercises and processes. It will bring about lasting changes that will resonate throughout your entire life. You'll be shining the light of your awareness on every aspect of your relationship with food, eating, your body, your perception of yourself and your relationship to others.

Although one little candle may not seem very powerful, you can, over time, light up and view every corner of your mind. Awareness is the first step to creating change. You will see what brought you to the place you are, learn how to love and accept yourself, and move on to achieve your goals based on that knowledge.

Eventually, when you are eating what you like and the weight begins to drop off, it will seem easy to simply live your life and experience peace with your body and food. Don't be in a rush to manifest the outward changes, though, because by doing that, you will be hooking yourself right back into the diet mentality of looking for the quick fix or magic bullet. The results can be dramatic, but they will occur slowly. As you change inwardly and start to heal your relationship to food, eating and your body, the outer manifestation will follow. Trust that. Your changing thoughts and beliefs about yourself will start to show in a variety of ways. People will begin to compliment you on your changing appearance even before you think there are any changes. Your self-esteem will increase, and you'll start seeing yourself in a different light.

Congratulate yourself on your courage to deal conclusively with your body, food and weight preoccupation. Get ready to embark on a fascinating journey, one that will forever change the way you relate to food and your body.

Since nagging yourself to lose weight didn't work, it's a good idea to be open to a new kind of strategy toward change. Along with many others who are loving themselves thin successfully, you'll be pleased with the results you can achieve. So let's get started.

TIP 1

Give Up Dieting Forever

The first step in finding freedom from dieting is to recognize that diets really don't work. The wisdom of not dieting will become obvious to you as we investigate this further. Most people consider dieting to be the only way to lose weight. But the odds are stacked against you, emotionally and physically.

Remember all the times that you've been on a diet. Perhaps you were successful and lost weight. In most cases, however, you didn't maintain the weight loss and you probably think it was something you did (or didn't do) that resulted in your failure to keep it off. The fact is the diet failed you. Once you went off the diet, you probably gained back all the weight you'd lost, plus a few pounds. In fact, this happens to 95-98% of people who do lose weight on a diet, so you're not alone. Diets have never worked in the long run and they never will. By their very nature, being "on a diet" implies that someday you will go off it. Let's look at the dynamics of dieting, and how they affect you adversely, both physically and emotionally.

Your body learns to function at the level of fewer calories, saving its fat stores for survival!

When you restrict caloric intake, your body is persuaded to burn its fat stores as fuel. You create an artificial environment of famine for yourself, and your body compensates by becoming thriftier with every calorie. Your metabolism, (the rate at which you burn food for your body's activities) slows down. This means that while initially you may lose pounds and some fat, you are training your body to function on less food and fewer calories. Everything else remaining equal, if you ever start eating more calories again, they will be stored as fat. You are training your body to burn fuel more slowly, saving the fat for survival. After going off the diet, you will regain fat faster than you did before you ever started dieting.

As discouraging as this may seem to you, it makes perfect sense from the point of view of your body. Being quite sophisticated intellectually, you know that you are probably not going to starve. People who feel they need to diet are surrounded by plenty. However, your body has not evolved to the point where it can distinguish "diet" from "starvation." So, when you self-impose famine in the form of a restrictive eating plan, your body holds on to its fat stores, and you burn your muscle fuel stores for your energy needs. Losing lean muscle mass through dieting further decreases your ability to burn calories, since your muscles can burn calories even while you're resting. So you gain weight more easily, even eating fewer calories. Dieting creates a vicious cycle of eating less, but gaining fat more easily from every morsel you do eat.

The "Yo-Yo" Effect

When you go off the diet and go back to eating a normal amount of food for your size and build, your body is relieved that the "famine" is over, and busily goes about storing more fat for the next period of "starvation."

This ability to store calories as fat is what has allowed our species to survive, much to the dismay of the repeat dieter, because it creates the "yo-yo" syndrome of weight loss and gain. The dieter finds it ever more difficult to lose weight as time goes by. Unless you find a way to increase the body's ability to burn fuel, through exercise, breathing or other means, the unfortunate result will usually be weight gain after quitting a diet.

Compulsive eating and self-loathing create a vicious downward spiral

In addition to the metabolic havoc that restrictive eating creates, dieting will bring an additional dismal and dysfunctional element to your life – compulsive eating and bingeing. Dieting and compulsive overeating are two sides of one coin, because dieting causes compulsive behavior through restriction and denial. How? Let's take a look.

The more restrictive a diet is, the more likely you'll indulge in bingeing. You can't deny yourself food; it's a necessity. If food serves a purpose for you other than satisfying hunger, then you will not be able to restrict yourself indefinitely from something you crave. Even if the diet initially is successful, and you lose weight, you're creating a "diet mentality". The diet mentality is the idea that restricting your food intake and losing a few pounds can solve all of your problems! If you lose weight, you think of yourself as "good." But what is on the other side of that coin? In most people's minds it means that if you don't lose weight or lose and gain the weight back, you are "bad." How do you think this affects your self-esteem?

Also, success at dieting allows you to avoid deeper issues that have contributed to your negative self-image in the first place. When you make the decision that "my body is somehow not right," weight loss brought about by dieting really is only a temporary bandage over feelings of low self-esteem, which will surface later in some form.

When you restrict your eating on a diet, there is a "rebound" effect that is both physical and emotional. You can control your eating for a certain amount of time, but then a "demon hunger" seems to take over, and you eat and eat as if you will never get enough.

So starts the vicious cycle of self-loathing, restriction, denial, shame and hope. We go on a diet, restrict our eating, lose control, gorge ourselves with food, feel self-loathing and disgust, feel ashamed, vow to do better, find a new diet, start the restricted eating plan again, lose self-control, etc. The destructive cycle goes on and on, resulting not in the thinner body that was the original intention of the diet, but rather a person who feels like an overweight failure, because they didn't have the "self-control" to make it work. The diet didn't solve anything and actually created many more problems. The unfortunate aspect of it all is the emotional, physical and psychological havoc created by an idea that doesn't really work in the first place.

The underlying dynamics of control

When you make your body wrong for being the way it is, and attempt to change your body through restricted eating, there can be several possible results.

One, you initially succeed at losing some excess weight, but when you go off the diet, you slowly but surely begin to gain it back. You feel disgusted with yourself.

Two, you can't stay on the diet, continually find yourself eating your "forbidden foods," lose respect for yourself because of your "lack of will power," beat yourself up, and vow to get greater control of yourself. The more you try to control yourself, the more "out of control" you feel. This only serves to make you even more upset and miserable, thinking of yourself as a failure, and you eat as a result of these feelings.

Three, you are successful at restricting your food intake and lose some weight. However, without food to use as a buffer against uncomfortable emotions, you feel negative feelings begin to surface. Subconscious fears start to come to the surface and cause you to make conclusions such as, "What's so important about being thin anyway?" or, "he/she only likes me for my body." You end up gaining back all the weight you've lost because you are sabotaged by your unresolved emotions.

What can you do? Give up dieting forever.

Give up the idea that the only way to create your ideal body is by restricting your eating and by eating what someone else says you should. You can achieve your ideal body through positive motivation to reach your goals and by being gentle, loving and nurturing with yourself. As you start to examine what you think is important in life (your values), you will make food choices and lifestyle changes based on positive choices about what you want for yourself. You want to love yourself and enjoy your life, right? You will learn to create the body you want based on those positive goals for yourself and giving yourself what you want, not only in the area of food or eating, but in the larger arena of your life. It is rare to achieve a positive outcome from a negative motivation; if that were possible, the most negative people would be the happiest, and life just doesn't work that way. Achieving your body goals, or any other goals for that matter, is always easier if you focus on your nearness to your goal, rather than on the relative distance.

Reading these pages, you will examine issues that have the potential to change your life. You will begin to see the reasons that you use food, and how that has served a purpose in your life. You can dramatically change your thoughts and behavior with regard to food, eating and your body. These shifts in consciousness and activities in turn will bring about changes in your body. As you realize that you deserve to pursue and have all the things you want in your life, your self-esteem will increase and your focus on food and eating will diminish. Food will not be as important to you, because you will not be restricting yourself and relating to food as "forbidden." Neither will you be using food to try to solve issues that can't be solved with food.

Since you are reading this information, some part of you has made the decision to learn about and heal your issues with food, eating and your body. Check in with your head and heart to ensure all parts of you are in alignment with this decision to choose freedom from dieting and all issues about food, eating and your body.

When you stop dieting, you will realize that you like being the one guiding your life, and that includes what and when you eat. Your appetites and desires are valid and should not be subject to the opinion of "diet experts" or anyone else. You will enjoy being the person who decides how to provide for your desires.

First, make the decision that you will never again punish yourself for the way you look by denying yourself food. Acknowledge where you are right now and take responsibility for your life and your body being the way it is. The best way to start making changes is to accept that reality. To use an old phrase, this is the first day of the rest of your life. You can start to make changes based on what you want for yourself, now and in the future, instead of being at the effect of the circumstances of your past. If you realize that you have been using food to avoid sexuality, for example – gaining weight to "armor" yourself against inappropriate remarks or to protect yourself against an abuser – heal your fears about sexuality, instead of using food to avoid the issue. I will show you how, but you must be willing to do the work. If you find you're not ready to do that, just acknowledge that you're not ready, and know that when you are ready, you will begin. Being honest with yourself is a necessity in uncovering and healing the reasons you use food to avoid your feelings.

The decision to stop dieting can be confronting and a little scary, but it is certainly a step in the right direction. This is the first step to eventually finding freedom from dieting and compulsive behavior.

A note about "Homeplay"

After every tip, there will be exercises, which will prompt you to think about your relationship to food, your emotions and what contributes to your dissatisfaction with your body. It's okay if you choose to do these now, or skip over them and start these exercises after you've read all the tips in this information. It's also okay for you never to do them. It's completely up to you. They are called "Homeplay" instead of homework, because I don't want you to relate to them as something that you HAVE to do, as you did in school. It's not bad not to do these exercises, just notice that you don't want to do them. There's nobody looking over your shoulder or grading you on these exercises; they are presented simply to give you further insights into yourself. Use them as tools for self-knowledge and to assist you in feeling stronger and better about yourself and your relationship to food and your body. At any point, stop reading and explore your feelings about the questions, and write your comments and feelings in your journal of personal discovery.

Homeplay

1. Your Childhood

Write down all you can remember about your relationship with food in your earliest years, such as, "As a child, I was _____around food," or "I ate everything that was offered to me," or "I was a finicky eater."

Was there not enough food or too much food?

Were one/both your parents always giving you food?

Did your grandparents provide different eating opportunities for you?

What were mealtime traditions?

What was the atmosphere like at mealtimes? (Cheerful, disciplined, tense)

What were your favorite foods?

What foods did you dislike?

Were you punished if you refused to eat them?

Find out all you can about your infancy and early childhood, regarding food. Look at pictures of yourself as an infant, to the age of about three years. Talk to your parents, if they are available, and ask them questions such as:

Was I breast or bottle-fed?

Did mother have any problems with breast-feeding?

Were there any other feeding problems?

Did I have allergies to formulas or foods?

Ask your mother what her relationship was like with your father, if possible, and vice versa.

Do you think your parents' relationship affected you?

How was your early childhood in general?

What were you like? Were you happy, good, rebellious, willful, lonely, stressed, etc.? Were you punished often? Write down notes on what you find and jot down your feelings about what you have learned.

If no one is available or no pictures can be located, you can still complete this assignment by finding a quiet place and relaxing, doing some deep breathing, and then allowing images of your childhood to arise in your mind. Be open to letting memories arise from your subconscious mind. Expect to have some feelings arise along with this self-questioning, and let yourself feel any emotions that may be connected to this process.

2. Self -Inquiry

Write out short answers, including any thoughts, beliefs or feelings that come up in response to the following statements:

How I feel about being overweight:

Some of the reasons I want to lose weight:

Why I think it is important for me to lose weight:

What I've tried to do in the past to lose weight:

What changes I could make in my life that would create weight loss:

If I was my perfect weight, I would be, or my life would be (write down any ideas that come up, not just your perfect numeric weight)

3. Deep Breathing/Relaxation

Twice a day, for at least five minutes each time, practice deep breathing and relaxation. Sit comfortably in a quiet spot. Focus on your incoming and outgoing breaths. Take a deep breath and as you exhale, concentrate on letting go of the muscles you can control, saying a word such as "relax," or just "aaahhh." Let go of any thoughts that arise and continue breathing and saying your word as you exhale. You may choose to schedule a time for this exercise, or just stop at various times during the day to do it.

4. Self-Assertiveness

Often overweight people or those with a negative self-image have difficulty setting boundaries around what they do for other people. Sometimes this stems from a desire to please others or be liked. Because of low self-esteem, they have difficulty putting their wants and needs before those of others', and this develops into resentment and negativity that can cause overeating. This exercise is to increase your assertiveness.

Begin to acknowledge to yourself that sometimes you feel like saying "no." This could be when someone asks you to do something, or when you have do something you don't want to do. Say "no" silently to yourself when you realize that you're facing something that you don't want. This allows you to acknowledge your ability to say no, and to increase within you the idea that your desires and preferences are at least as important as those of others.

This week, say "no" silently to yourself as often as you feel like it. This can also be phrased as, "I don't want to" and "I won't." If you become aware there is something that needs to be done that you don't want to do, say that to yourself. Acknowledge that there's a conflict between what you want and what must be done. If it really needs to be done, you will do it anyway. The important thing is to hear yourself say, "No, I would prefer not."

Acknowledge that, "No, I don't want to get up now," "I don't want to go to work," "I don't want to do the dishes." If traffic is a hassle, express it by saying, "I don't want to drive in this traffic. I don't want to hunt for parking," When you feel overwhelmed by your list of things to do, say, "I don't want to do what I am supposed to do." Because we often suppress our own desires out of a need to feel liked and accepted, we use food and eating as a means of "stuffing down" our feelings of frustration and/or anger. This exercise gives you practice in saying, "I don't want to be a good girl and hide my feelings."

Say "no" to things you know you have to do, but have been putting off. Just tell yourself that you don't feel like doing them. Get honest. Acknowledge to yourself what you do and don't want in your life. This helps you to sort out your values and learn what is right for you. By letting go of the "shoulds," you are making your own desires clearer.

TIP 2

MAKE IT OKAY TO EAT
ANY KIND OF FOOD

D oes the following strike a chord of recognition? You feel like your life would be better if you lost a few pounds, so you decide to go on a diet.

The diet requires that you restrict yourself from eating many of the foods you love. After a few days of restricted eating, you may notice that certain foods start to become more important to you, to loom larger in your imagination. You crave them intensely. Whatever your favorite foods may be, when you tell yourself you can't have them, they start to occupy a much greater than normal place in your awareness. In fact, you will probably find yourself obsessing about foods that aren't even your favorites.

When you are on a diet, you spend a great deal of your time thinking about food, looking forward to eating, wishing it was time to eat the next meal, obsessing about the candy bar you can't have, and generally being preoccupied with eating. Food becomes the "forbidden fruit," because anything that you or anyone else says you can't have, you naturally want and crave. Tension arises because you feel conflicted about eating. Much of your time and energy is used in this endless cycle of negative thinking about what you "should" and "shouldn't" be eating. In addition, by being on a self-imposed diet plan, you're constantly reminding yourself that you're not okay the way you are, and this detracts from your sense of well-being.

You find yourself thinking about food and its effect on your body most of the time, whether it is beating yourself up for how you broke the "rules" during your last meal, thinking about how hungry you are, about what you "get" to eat at the next meal, or what you will look like if you are successful on your diet. Your day is filled with struggle. You wrestle with staying on the diet. You deny that you are hungry. You probably notice yourself thinking of eating often during the day, because you are ignoring something about yourself that needs attention. You flirt with the idea of how to "cheat" on your diet and still get the results you want. Instead of being a means of enjoyably satisfying yourself and nourishing your body, food takes on a personality of its own. Your hunger threatens to sabotage you at every turn. Food becomes the "enemy," something to be feared and avoided. It can't be trusted, and you start to relate to food as if it can do bad things to you without your consent.

Thus, eating becomes dangerous. You become obsessed with food and every time you go to nourish yourself, you are waging a battle. Which will win – your appetite or your will power? Even if you are victorious in controlling your appetite at a particular meal, there's always the danger of losing control at dinner with friends, a sumptuous buffet at a party, meeting someone for coffee, or at that cute little donut shop down the street, beckoning to you to fill that void, threatening to undo your best efforts.

You can see how this takes up much of your time and energy better spent elsewhere. This is not an enjoyable way to live, yet dieters endure these conflicts daily.

Does the scenario sound familiar? By going on a restricted eating plan and denying yourself the foods you love and crave, you create an obsessive relationship with those foods. This sets the stage for a lifetime of struggle with eating and your body. You create an intense longing for all kinds of foods that no amount of cottage cheese or carrot sticks can ever satisfy.

So food becomes both exciting and dangerous, the "forbidden

fruit" that you flirt with and perhaps use to distract yourself from other issues in your life. You neglect developing yourself in other ways to become a full and complete human being because you think that if you are the "right" size, everything else will magically be okay. Food keeps you focused on your body as an object and distances you from other important areas of your life. You can talk endlessly with your friends about food, dieting, and exercise, but it doesn't help you solve your negative issues with your body. Dieting becomes an end in itself, where you feel successful if you lose weight, and despair if you don't.

Here's an exercise:

Imagine that your body size and shape are frozen in time. There is nothing that you or anyone else can do to change his or her body. Everyone stays the way they are right now for their entire life. You can't work out to grow more muscle or burn fat, and there is no such thing as dieting to change your body size. You simply have the body you're given. Now finish the following statements:

If I could never change my body size or shape –

I would do these things the same as I do now:

What I would do differently:

Ways in which I would develop myself to create fulfillment and happiness:

Never being able to change my body makes me feel:

Homeplay

1. Childhood research

Continue your research by asking questions, finding pictures, and remembering events. In addition, find a child to observe – one of your own, a grandchild or a relative. Spend an hour at a park, playground or other place where a number of small children are interacting with their parents.

Observe them and notice how they relate to their parents, how they operate both dependently and independently, whether or not they have anything to eat, and if so, how they interact with food and how their parents relate with them.

Try to imagine what you were like at that age and how your interactions with your parents and with food might have been.

2. Deep breathing/Progressive muscle relaxation

Twice a day, for five minutes each time, practice deep breathing, while mentally going through your body and suggesting to your various body parts it's possible to relax. Even if you feel awkward doing this, do the best you can. Notice if any parts of your body seem especially resistant to relaxation or dense with tension or feeling. You may choose to schedule a time for this exercise, or stop at particularly stressful moments during the day to do it.

3. Assertiveness

You are learning to say "no" in a positive and healthy way. Tell a friend or family member that you are learning to assert yourself and ask them if they will be willing to participate in an experiment. If they agree, ask them if it would be all right with them for you to say "no" this week to something they ask you for, and that you will then discuss with them whether or not you are willing to do it anyway. Practice your ability to say "no."

TIP 3

RELEARN HOW TO EAT

You eat for all kinds of reasons other than hunger, and it may be interesting to understand how this has served you in many ways. You eat to be social – since the dawn of time, mealtimes are also family gathering times. You eat when you're in pain, to soothe or sedate yourself. You eat to celebrate events, and you eat to reward yourself. Can you remember if you've ever used food as a reward for putting in a long day's work? So food nurtures you in ways that are very primal.

Even people who aren't compulsive overeaters sometimes eat when they're not hungry, for a variety of reasons. If you've allowed yourself to get overly hungry, you may eat too fast, and this can cause you to overeat. Or you may try to use food to boost your energy when you're tired or bored. However, when you habitually use food to change your experience, or to avoid certain feelings, it's not healthy. By becoming aware of the ways that you might be using food, you can start to overcome "using" food for problems food can't solve. You may notice that you eat to avoid feeling emotional pain. When you understand that the way you eat is not helping you create the body you want, take responsibility for that. Not to blame yourself, but just to notice. Start looking at the ways in which you use food to fix the feelings that you label "hunger."

Many compulsive eaters never allow themselves to feel real hunger. They just eat all the time. They eat by the clock, thinking "It's noon, so I must be hungry for lunch," instead of waiting for their bodies to signal them that they have used up the fuel from the previous meal and they need more. Sometimes people eat as preventative maintenance. They eat because they think they might be hungry later. Eating when you're not really hungry is like trying to top off your gas tank when you don't need gas. In your car the excess fuel would spill out, but in your body the excess food gets stored as fat.

Some people feel guilty if they don't want to eat food that is being offered, so they eat it anyway, hungry or not. In certain cultures, it's completely normal to eat when you're not hungry, as in "What? You have to be hungry to eat? Since when?" Many people eat when they want to "be good" to or treat themselves. If they feel sad, lonely, or want to avoid feelings of boredom, food acts as a comforting friend. Food can act as a sedative and soothe you when you're feeling angry or upset. Bingeing and its aftermath of self-hatred can effectively distract you and keep you from dealing effectively with a situation in which you're undecided about what to do.

But food doesn't really solve any of these feelings or states of consciousness; it just temporarily changes your experience. Eating or bingeing buffers you from the pain or intensity of your feelings in the moment, but in the long run, creates more problems.

If you think about it, you can probably think of a few times that you've eaten when you weren't hungry, as we all have. To help you clarify this idea, finish the following statements:

Sometimes I eat when I'm feeling:

I feel especially hungry when:

I usually seek out something to eat when I feel:

The last time I ate when I was (shy, bored, lonely, excited, angry) was:

It's especially important to be gentle with yourself about this. The reason you use food is because you don't know what else to do with the uncomfortable feelings. You could use something a lot more destructive, like alcohol or drugs. So until now, food has been one of the best tools you've had to deal with unresolved emotions, and that's why you "use" food for a variety of reasons other than hunger. As you go along, you'll be learning effective and healthy tools to help you cope with your emotions, so you can use food for what it is meant to do, nourish your body.

Is this feeling really hunger, or what?

Sometimes you feel something in your body that you assume is "hunger," because in the past, food has helped to relieve it. But is it really hunger? Is it really your body requesting food in order to fuel its functions? Are you really, truly "hungry" all the time, as you may think you are? If you are a compulsive overeater or use food to avoid feeling emotions, you probably call many feelings "hunger" that are actually something else, like boredom, sadness, awkwardness or feelings of inadequacy or emptiness. Since you have habitually used food to make these feelings go away, it is natural to relate to them as "hunger." Without blaming yourself or making yourself wrong, can you recall a time when you ate when you weren't really hungry because it relieved tension of some sort?

Briefly write about it:

Because food has such deep and primal associations with survival, eating when you are not hungry gives instant relief from the immediate fear or negative emotion, but it's never enough. It doesn't really do the trick. The same "fix" works less well over time, so we eat more and more often. We keep raising the ante. It's the same with all addictions and compulsive behavior – it takes more and more to give some relief, but it's never enough to heal the hurt.

"Being with" your feelings

How do you begin to get in touch of the entire range of emotions that can exist at times when you think you're feeling hunger? You can begin by recognizing that emotions can cause the desire to eat, masquerading as hunger. Start to pay attention to your internal cues. This means focusing on the feelings in your body to determine if what you are feeling is hunger or some other feeling that can't be "fixed" by food.

In order to do this, let yourself feel the feelings in your body that you normally would feed in order to make the feelings go away. Instead of going immediately for food, pause (even if only for one moment) and ask yourself,

Am I feeling hunger, is my stomach empty, or is this something else?

Am I feeling excitement or happiness?

Do I need to tell someone something?

Am I upset?

Do I need to call a friend for some support and encouragement?

Am I feeling angry?

Do I want to cry?

Do I want a hot bath or a hug?

Do I feel deserving of a reward?

Am I eating to please someone else?

You won't always be able to tell exactly what is going on with you at the moment. But as you begin to allow yourself to discriminate between the feelings, just for a couple of minutes, the next time you feel like eating, you will see that it may not be hunger after all. You may be surprised at how quickly you start being able to distinguish between feelings of boredom, anger, sadness, and real "stomach-being-empty" hunger. As you start to get in touch with your natural sensations of hunger, you will find that you won't need to eat every time you feel something in your body. You will begin to recognize that certain feelings can't be healed by food, food only covers them up temporarily. The feelings will still be there after you've eaten, so using food is really only a momentary distraction. Give yourself some time to find the feeling that is asking for attention, and "be with" that feeling by doing some deep breathing and relaxation when you're experiencing it.

Acknowledge, allow, and accept

Many times I've had the urge to eat candy when I was feeling frustrated or unmotivated to work. I now know that the feeling of wanting candy is emotions masquerading as hunger. Instead of immediately going for the "quick food fix," I spend some time exploring the urge. I look for a way to soothe myself by giving myself compassion and permission to have that feeling. I tell myself that I understand and accept myself, even if that understanding and acceptance aren't perfect. When I experience a negative emotion, there's probably a good reason I feel as I do.

So begin to make it a habit to be on your own side. Don't immediately make the feeling wrong or try to make it go away. Notice that you would probably have compassion for someone else if they told you about it, so have compassion for yourself.

Feelings are constantly flowing

Stop being down on yourself for having a feeling, and the feeling with which you're struggling will begin to loosen its grip on you. By learning to "be with" them, you will soon start to notice that the feelings are patterns of energy that can flow through you without your needing to do anything to make them go away.

Some statements that you might say to yourself –

I'm open to this feeling teaching me something about myself.

The feeling I'm having is very human – I guess I'm pretty normal.

I'm really glad this feeling isn't worse.

I can relax even with this feeling.

Isn't it amusing that this feeling usually causes me to want to eat?

What a curious experience it is to notice that this feeling makes me want to eat.

Some statements that might be particularly effective for me when I'm feeling like I want to eat, but I know I'm not hungry are:

"Legalizing food" and eating what you want

As a dieter, for as long as you can remember, certain foods have probably been off-limits to you. Indeed, you've most likely permanently excluded whole food groups, including fats and sugars. However, have the "forbidden foods" somehow found their way into your mouth? So you may notice that, even with the best of intentions to abstain, the something in you that craves those foods demands to be fed. By telling yourself that you can't have it, you practically guarantee that you will eat it. I know it sounds crazy, but that's the truth with many dieters. Legalizing food will change all of that by allowing you to get out of the way of your own desires.

What does that mean? Legalizing food means making any food okay to eat. It means taking all foods off the forbidden list and thereby eventually removing their power over you. If you are dealing with a charging bull, does it make sense to stand squarely in front of it and demand that it stop? Or to step aside and, like a skillful matador, allow it to thunder past? You may be covered with dust, but you'll still be standing. Legalizing food is like being a skillful matador with your food cravings – you allow them to exist, and respect them, and eventually they won't knock you for a loop.

Legalizing food means that it's okay to eat anything you want, as long as it's exactly what you want and you are hungry. All food is legal

"I can have it, but do I really WANT it?"

Give yourself the time to make the transition into allowing yourself to eat any and all foods. The truth about this is that you really can eat only so much cookie dough or candy bars before making yourself sick. Eventually your body says, "Okay, I've had enough chocolate cake, I don't want any more right now." When you begin to realize that you can have chocolate cake whenever you want it, you don't crave it as much. As you begin to heal your compulsive eating behavior, you will begin to make the "right" food choices, based on your values for yourself and what you consider to be healthy foods. You will be able to say, "Of course, I know I can have it, but is it really what I feel like eating?" Only after allowing yourself to go through a period of "outrageous" eating, can you get past the denial of giving yourself the foods you want and crave, and healing your food addiction. This is the way to freedom regarding food and eating. For many, this approach has been the way out of compulsive behavior and self-abuse. It reduces your fear and anxiety about food, and when you're less anxious, you will eat less.

No food is "off limits"

The wonderful part is that as you go through all of your formerly "forbidden foods" in this way, eventually you start to realize that you can have them whenever you desire, and you don't crave them as much. The part of you that has been deprived of satisfaction from eating begins to learn that it will no longer be deprived of the foods you love. You relax and eventually will be satisfied eating appropriate amounts of your favorite foods in a way that will allow you to be satisfied with less, and lose weight. You will have the satisfaction of eating and feeling fed by exactly the foods that you love the most. This lessens your compulsiveness and anxiety about eating and you will eat less. There is no reason to be compulsive about the foods that you know you can have. Allow yourself some time for this to occur, and be patient with yourself as it is happening.

However, watch what your mind does with this concept. Be aware of the way you think about this way of feeding yourself. This is not a recommendation for eating everything in sight. You must learn and follow the Eating Guidelines, explained in Tip 6. Your goal is not mindless gluttony. Ending food addiction is about increasing your awareness about your relationship to food and eating. You are in the process of becoming a connoisseur. It's the beginning of relating to food in a completely new way. The idea is to be able to tell yourself, "I know I *can* have it. Do I really want it, or is it because I thought I couldn't have it that I want it?"

This is a process of nurturing yourself. Be patient, and expect thoughts like, "I shouldn't be doing this," or "This is bad for me," to arise. These thoughts are normal for chronic dieters. Stop for a moment and consider what you are doing for yourself. Remind yourself that you are trying something different, because what you did in the past didn't work. Again, patience is necessary.

EXERCISE

Some of the things you might say to yourself are:

This is what my body wants, I'm taking care of myself.

I'm being good to myself, I'm nurturing and nourishing myself.

I'm taking care of what the hungry child in me wants and craves, and through this process of feeding myself what I want, I am healing myself.

Whenever you hear yourself say, "This really isn't okay," let that thought be the motivation to counter it with a positive message of, "I'm trying a new approach to loving and taking care of myself."

As time goes on, and you continue to feed yourself what you desire, it will seem more and more natural for you to eat what you want and not give yourself any negative messages. You will simply pay attention to what you want to eat, and give yourself that. Ask yourself, "What is it I really want to eat in this moment?" instead of putting just anything in your body. At times you will feel as if you're starving and you'll want to eat whatever is easiest. But more and more, you will develop an awareness of what you want the most in any given moment, and feed yourself exactly the right food for your own satisfaction.

By feeding yourself the foods you really love, you are giving yourself the message that it is okay to have your desires, and that you're okay the way you are. This allows your self-esteem to rise and gives you the positive motivation to reach your goal of having your ideal body. Also, you will be aware of how your food choices affect you with regard to your goals for yourself. When you know you can have a certain food, you have the choice to decide if eating it helps you move toward your goals for your body. Sometimes people see reaching their goal of a perfect body isn't really important in order to have an enjoyable life. As you calm down about your relationship to food and feel better about yourself as you are, you will naturally enjoy all of your life more.

The choice is always yours, whether you want to experience the food in your mouth or the satisfaction of doing the things you have decided support your goals, such as eating in a certain way. The important thing is that YOU approve of your choice and support yourself in making it. Tell yourself, "I've decided to have this dessert, so I might as well enjoy it thoroughly, rather than making myself wrong for it."

In the homeplay section, write what foods you eat and when, and how you felt when you were eating it, especially if it is a "formerly forbidden food." Also note why you think you chose that particular food, and see if that relates to anything in your past.

One of the major benefits that come from this idea of eating what you want, when you want it, is having a lot less anxiety about food. When you are taking care of yourself, you will experience less stress. Thus, as you relax about the idea of controlling yourself, you will actually eat less.

Homeplay

1. Examining Your Ideas and Beliefs About Food

What messages have you received about food from your family?

From society?

What are the messages you received as a child about food?

Were you poor or did you get the feeling that there was never going to be enough food?

Were you told you needed to clean you plate before you could leave the table or before you could have dessert?

Were you told there are starving children in India, so you must eat all of your dinner?

How do these messages affect you?

Other family messages were or are:

Were there different rules for you and your siblings?

What were the phrases or things you were told about your body when you were growing up?

How are these messages still affecting you as an adult? For example, do you notice that you feel compelled to eat everything on your plate in a restaurant because it would be a waste of money if you didn't? Or that you must eat everything offered you when you are a guest for dinner because to do otherwise would be rude and insulting to your host? To explore this further, finish the following statement:

Sometimes I eat even when I'm not hungry because:

_____

Do you find that you stuff your feelings down with food because it's not okay to be angry? Or do you eat to soothe yourself when you're feeling particularly anxious? Write about it in your journal.

Pay attention and be aware if and when you overeat and ask yourself if there is an early childhood message playing in your head.

2. *"Being with" your feelings*

When you notice that you are having an uncomfortable feeling that makes you feel anxious or upset, try to just "be with" that feeling a little bit longer than you normally would before doing whatever it is that you do to deal with that feeling. For example, if you feel anxious or stressed out and you normally would make a trip to the vending machine to get a snack, let yourself "be with" the feeling of wanting that snack, and wait a few moments before getting it. Take a few deep breaths, relax, and let yourself feel the feeling. See if the feeling changes while you're paying attention to it. Don't restrict yourself from having the snack; just delay it for a few moments while you inwardly explore your desire.

What happened when I tried this technique:

_____

3. *Assertiveness*

Learn to say "no" in a positive and healthy way to other people. Notice how you feel about each request someone makes of you. If it is something that you strongly do not want to do, refuse to do it. Then negotiate with the person who made the request, so that either the task gets done some other way (if necessary), or both of you are satisfied even if the task does not get done.

For example, someone in your household asks you to run an errand for them and you don't want to because you are tired and want to stay home. Say, "No, thanks, I'll pass. Perhaps you can ask someone else. I am tired now and want to rest." Find out if there is any reason that they cannot do it themselves. If they cannot, find out if it can be done later and who can do it. If it needs to be done right away, see if you can find a way the person can be satisfied even if you don't do it. Remember, there is often more than one solution to any situation.

How I used this technique this week and what happened:

_____

_____

_____

4. Food

Allow yourself to eat what you want, as much as you want, whenever you want. Make sure you are not stopping because you think you should or because you're afraid you'll gain weight. Stop only when you feel satisfied. Pay attention – if you get to a point where you think you've had enough, relax for a moment and assess your level of satisfaction. Then if you still want to eat some more, go ahead. The important thing is for you to make sure you don't accidentally deprive yourself.

Some of my formerly forbidden foods that I ate this week were:

_____

_____

How I felt eating my formerly forbidden food:

_____

_____

5. This week:

Eat when you are hungry.

Eat exactly what you want to eat.

Eat until you are satisfied.

Don't stuff yourself mindlessly. Eat with awareness of how the food tastes and feels in your mouth and in your stomach.

If you find yourself overeating, see if you can notice why you overeat. What messages do you give yourself when you overeat? What happened during the day on which you overate?

Try to be more gentle and compassionate with yourself than you have been in the past.

I overate on (fill in day) _____ because:

_____

_____

6. *Compassion and understanding for myself this week:*

None, I felt upset with myself.

A little, I could understand my behavior.

It was okay with me, I felt compassionate towards myself.

A lot, I felt I nurtured my desires and myself.

TIP 4

KNOWING WHAT FOODS
YOU WANT AND NEED

One of the most interesting and profound exercises for you to do with your new way of feeding yourself is to write out a shopping list. This means you start to think about and write down all of your favorite and/or formerly forbidden foods. This list will probably be unlike any other shopping list you've ever written. Why? Because you will be reaching back into your past and considering any and all of the foods or snacks that you've ever loved or wanted. Put them on your list. It doesn't even matter if they're currently available. You may not be able to find some items, but you're developing the idea that you can have anything you want, so put it on your list. No food is off limits to you. This is a process of allowing yourself the freedom to create the mindset, "I CAN have it, do I really want it?" instead of your usual idea, "I CAN'T have it."

Remembering that this is a learning and healing process for you, take your list to the market, go into all the aisles that you used to avoid, and purchase as many of the items on your list as you want.

You should expect to feel some anxiety when confronting your taboos about what foods you should eat. You'll hear yourself saying things like, "This can't possibly work. What am I doing?" Also, fears about what people are thinking will come up, but don't let these ideas or fears stop you from going through with this process. Consider this an awareness-expanding field trip. Nurture yourself with thoughts of, "I'm being good to my body and feeding it what it wants to heal years of denial," and "This is how I'm healing my addiction to food." Be sure you bring home plenty of your favorite foods, because you don't want to run out. You should fill your cupboards with all the foods that you've always longed for, but rarely dared to buy or take home. Bring home much more of the formerly forbidden foods that you can possibly eat. Your thought, when surrounded by all of your favorite foods, won't be, "Should I eat it" but "Which of my favorite foods shall I eat?"

This is a very powerful process. It will give you amazing insights into your relationship to food, eating and your body. Again, if you feel fearful, or self-conscious, just notice that and don't allow those feelings to get in the way of doing the process.

This is about making peace with food. It is about learning to live with your desires, not denying them and trying to make them go away as you've done in the past. The feeling and idea that you will create is that you know you can have whatever you want, and that it's going to be available for you whenever you want. Over time, as you experience your ability to satisfy yourself with the foods you really crave, your body will naturally ask for a wide variety of foods. It may be cake or it may be salad. It makes no difference, you simply give your body what it is asking for, and you leave behind forever the pain of deprivation.

Yummy or yucky – you decide

You will be amazed that, legalizing foods, and developing the mindset of "I *can* have it," will remove much of the charge of eating any food. You'll either eat it and say, "Gee, this is what I've been craving and denying myself all these years? I don't even like it that much!," or you'll say, "AAAHHH!" and will be deeply satisfied regarding that particular food. Either way, you will learn something about your relationship to that food and will have lessened your compulsive relationship to food in general. When you legalize all food, it allows you to either have it or not. Part of the reason that you stuff yourself on a binge is that you think you are not supposed to have it, you can never have it again, and that this food will never be available to you. When you are feeding yourself your desired foods on demand, there will come a point when your body will say, "Okay, this is enough." You learn that your formerly forbidden foods will never be disallowed again. Your eating habits will begin to change. You will know that if you want a certain food, it will always be available to you, and this knowledge will lessen your compulsiveness.

After some time allowing yourself to have any food you want, you will either choose to eat it or not. When you get to the point of knowing you can have anything, you start to honor yourself with your food choices. When you can say, "I can have that," the next question becomes, "Do I really want that? How will I feel eating it and how will my body respond to that?" Think about the feeling that you'll have after eating it and make your choice accordingly.

What about my allergies?

Many people ask me, "I love and crave chocolate, but I have an allergic reaction to it, what should I do?" The answer is, be aware that you'll have a reaction to it and decide whether you want to experience that reaction. Take control by recognizing that it is your choice, don't give control to the food. You will either say, "I don't care, I want the chocolate anyway," or "Oh yeah, I remember I got a rash the last time I ate chocolate, I don't want to feel that today, maybe I'll pass." You make choices based on what you like to experience more – the taste of chocolate in your mouth or feeling good by not having an allergic reaction. If you decide to eat the chocolate and have a reaction, be gentle with yourself and say, "Well, today I felt like eating the chocolate. Maybe next time, I'll choose differently." Don't make yourself wrong for eating the chocolate, just notice that you're not ready to let go of it, and know that you will when you are ready. You see, when you don't resist your desires, you have the option to take responsibility for the effect the food has on you. Based on self-love and respect, you don't want to create discomfort or self-loathing. Perhaps that is the way you related to yourself in the past, but no longer.

It's all about choice

We all have certain foods for which we have an intolerance or that don't agree with us, foods that have certain consequences, and yet the forbidden nature of these foods keeps us eating them. If you stop and think about what the food will feel like in your body after you've eaten it, you may want to say, "Well yes, I know I can have it, but do I really want to feel the way I know that I will feel, having eaten that cheese pizza?" (Or chocolate cake, pint of ice cream, six doughnuts, bag of chips, etc.) Not that there is anything wrong with the food itself. Any food can have a place in your diet. You just want to look beyond the immediate gratification of the moment, and know that the food will have an effect on you with which you have not been very pleased or happy in the past.

Part of you may say, "I don't care. I just want it." And that's fine. That is the part that needs to feel satisfied before you can let go of compulsive eating. Continue being gentle and patient with yourself. Relate to this as a learning process. Realize that you have been entertaining certain thoughts about foods, and that these beliefs will not disappear overnight.

Homeplay

1. *What do you want?*

Every time you have a wish or a brief thought about something you want, write it down. Write down anything, from any area of your life (not just body goals), no matter how outrageous or impossible it seems to you. It could be something small or large; it doesn't have to be practical at all. Don't edit yourself – write whatever you feel. It is most important to let yourself know what you want. Also, pay attention to your feelings. Maybe you wish a certain person would treat you differently, or that this person was not around. Or maybe you want a hug or to escape work and go for a walk. Whatever it is, capture it and write it down.

Some of the things I want right now are:

_____

_____

_____

_____

_____

2. *Expressing emotions*

Take some time right now to relax and think about some of the messages you've been given and beliefs you have about emotional expression and feelings. What messages did you receive about feelings and the expression of feelings?

By your parents?

By siblings?

By teachers?

By society?

How are these messages still affecting you as an adult?

Do you find it difficult to express certain feelings?

Is it hard even to know what you are feeling?

Are you afraid of being made fun of or criticized for what you feel?

Do you feel you deserve to have your emotional needs met?

Pay attention when you are interacting with others and ask yourself what old messages or beliefs are still playing in your head.

This Week:

Eat when you are hungry.

Eat whatever you want to eat.

Eat until you are satisfied.

If you overeat this week, notice your thoughts and feelings about it and write them down here:

Why did you overeat?

What messages do you give yourself either while you're eating or after?

What was going on for you before you overate?

Can you be gentle and forgiving with yourself?

Which best describes your compassion level toward yourself?

None, I felt upset with myself

A little, I could understand my behavior

It was okay with me, I felt compassionate towards myself

A lot, I felt I nurtured myself and my desires

HOW EMOTIONS MASQUERADE AS HUNGER

You feel your emotions all over

In the process of life, things happen about which we don't know how to feel okay. Situations arise and some feelings can be so uncomfortable that we need to learn to ignore them, so as not to feel the pain that is connected to them. In other words, we suppress these uncomfortable feelings to buffer ourselves from the discomfort. Sometimes the pain threatens to become overwhelming and we avoid it by indulging in behavior that will keep the feelings suppressed, such as drinking alcohol, taking drugs, watching a lot of television, compulsive sex or shopping. Some people go through life trying to keep their feelings suppressed. But the feelings are still there, waiting to be reactivated every time a similar situation arises.

There is a different way to relate to your feelings, though, which we will be learning in a later tip. That is, you will learn to heal them so they no longer govern your behavior. Rather than try to avoid the feelings, we seek to change the way we relate to them so that they do not cause us discomfort. That discomfort is what forces us into suppressive behavior, including overeating.

Any suppressive behavior will do

If you are living with unresolved issues from your past, the feelings remain in your body until you resolve the negativity regarding that experience. When the negativity gets integrated, the feelings will no longer cause you to act in ways that detract from your sense of well-being. Until then, however, you will continue to use whatever it takes to keep you from being aware of and experiencing the negativity stored in your body.

How your feelings affect your behavior

For example, in relation to compulsive overeating, anyone having unresolved feelings of guilt or fear regarding sex may not want to get thinner. Being their ideal weight would make them more attractive and gain unwanted attention. Being thinner would force them to confront the issue of sexual attractiveness, which they may not have the skills to deal with. Or, they may be afraid of acting promiscuous if they were thin and attractive. Looking good and getting attention may bring up such uncomfortable feelings that they use food or being heavy to buffer themselves from the world and literally cushion themselves from the pain of exposure.

Feelings affect you in other ways, too. Let's say your mother has always encouraged you to eat. Every time she invites you over to dinner, you eat more than you want. Perhaps you are afraid to refuse the food she offers, for fear that she will be upset with you. You are afraid of her disapproval. So you continue to overeat in her presence, because of unresolved feelings or fear. By eating more food than you normally would, you avoid feeling your conflicted emotions about your mother.

Here's another example: If you have an argument with your mate, and you feel anger, resentment, and frustration, you might have the urge for an ice cream sundae. Indulging in that sundae, you might never get to resolve those feelings of frustration, which you are avoiding by eating the ice cream sundae. Eating serves to suppress your feelings. However, by allowing yourself to experience the feelings of anger, resentment and frustration, you would be more in a position to do something about them. By blocking the feeling of anger with eating, you allow your feelings to dictate your actions. So the feelings never get resolved. They simply get suppressed, and are waiting to be activated the next time something or someone pushes your buttons.

When we are aware of the feelings, we have the option of acting on them directly to resolve and heal them. However, sometimes we don't know what the feelings are. As compulsive overeaters, we tend to experience all of our feelings, even pleasure and excitement, as hunger.

What IS this I'm feeling?

Begin to slow down, and notice what you're feeling. You may have an automatic habit of putting something in your mouth as soon as you feel anything. Start to distinguish between feelings of hunger and the entire range of other feelings, including sadness, anger, boredom, lust, rage and joy. Because, even though food may do a good job of temporarily suppressing or covering up other feelings, the only feeling that food can solve is hunger.

In order to learn to distinguish between hunger and the many other feelings that you have throughout the day, you will begin to pay more attention to every feeling, exploring and allowing yourself to feel it, even for just one moment. Don't run away. Determine what it is you're hungry for. If it isn't food, you can start seeking out what will really satisfy that need. Pay attention, and soon you will be able to distinguish between physical hunger and emotional feelings.

Start tuning in to your body in a different way, an open and loving way. Ask your body what it needs right now, and be open to any kind of an answer. Your body might say, "I need a hot bath," or "I feel like crying." It might be a mixture of feelings. You might be experiencing emotions related to something that happened that day. Of course, the feeling may actually be hunger, but by slowing down and letting yourself experience whatever feelings are there, you learn to identify the feelings and not lump them all together under the heading of hunger. Don't be judgmental of yourself. Allow the feeling to be there.

Homeplay

1. Using your weight as protection

Examine the ways in which you use extra weight as protection. Write out responses to the following statements.

I feel safer when I am heavier because:

When I am thin I feel less safe because:

In general, when I'm carrying extra weight, people treat me:

_____

_____

When I am thin, people treat me:

_____

_____

When I am thinner they...

_____

_____

Men/women respond to me: (choose the opposite of your sex)

_____

Men/women respond to me: (choose the same sex)

_____

Ways in which I feel more comfortable with extra weight...
Around men:

_____

Around women:

_____

_____

If I were thinner I would feel threatened by:

_____

If I were thinner I would be afraid of:

_____

If I were thinner I would be uncomfortable with:

_____

2. Examining emotional pain

Recall and write down a time in the last week or so when you ate as a result of, or to suppress, emotional pain.

What were you afraid would happen if you allowed yourself to feel the pain, hurt or sadness?

Were you afraid you would cry all day, sleep all day, not go to work, run out of the room screaming, or injure someone or yourself?

As a result of eating, what happened to the pain?

Did you forget about it?

Did it go away?

Did it get worse?

Did you feel better or worse afterwards?

Write out some alternatives for yourself for dealing with pain. For example, find a private space and cry, hug yourself, talk to a friend, beat a pillow, listen to your favorite music, take a bath, get a massage, or do some deep breathing.

3. Self-examination in the mirror

This exercise is done for the purpose of learning to accept yourself, the way you are right now. Self-acceptance is the basis for positive change. You're not doing this to compare yourself to others and end up feeling like a failure one more time. If you find yourself being negative about how you look, stop and do this at another time. Accepting yourself as you are now does not mean that you "give up," or stop trying to improve yourself, it means that you accept the reality of where you are now. This allows you to take responsibility for your choices in the past, and start with an entirely new perspective, from today forward.

EXERCISE

Gaze at yourself in a full-length mirror. Describe yourself, as if you were telling someone else about you. Use descriptive, non-judgmental statements, such as, "I curve here and this area goes in. I have such-and-such color eyes, and short blond hair. This area here is hard, and this area is soft." Do this exercise only if you can maintain a non-judgmental perspective. If you find yourself saying negative statements, stop and try it again another time.

5. *This week:*

Eat when you are hungry.

Eat exactly what you want to eat.

Eat until you are satisfied.

Don't stuff yourself mindlessly. Eat with awareness of how the food tastes and feels in your mouth and in your stomach.

EAT WHEN YOU'RE HUNGRY, STOP WHEN YOU'RE FULL

Feeding Yourself on Demand

One of the more unusual aspects of this program is that you learn to honor your own uniqueness regarding what and when you want to eat. For a long time, you may have been making yourself rigidly conform to a diet regime that is completely different from the way you really like to eat. For example, some people aren't hungry in the morning when they wake up. But some diet programs dictate eating breakfast whether you want to or not. The issue here is not whether breakfast is good for you, but that if you don't want it, you're not going to be successful on a diet that states you must have it. Not to mention that many of these diets don't honor the fact that we all have completely individual preferences.

When you are practicing eating whatever you want when you want it, remember to tune in and listen to what your body is asking to be fed. If your body is asking for a hamburger and fries and you give it Caesar salad, you'll still be unsatisfied. You can never get enough of that which you don't really want. Think about this example – if you are feeling that you'd like to taste and have something in your stomach like a cheese omelet, no amount of crackers or pickles will satisfy that desire. Trying to fill your hunger with the wrong food will result in eating more food and experiencing less satisfaction. In other words, if you're trying to satisfy yourself with something that your body isn't really hungry for, you'll eat more than you need trying to get full. If you give yourself the food that you're craving and it is exactly what you want, you will find that you will be able to eat less and be satisfied.

Eat when you're hungry, stop when you're full

I've been asking you to eat whatever you want whenever you want it. The next step is to focus on your feelings of hunger. Yes, that's right! Exactly what you've been trying to avoid feeling for so long, your hunger. Because of anxiety regarding food and eating, many people never let themselves feel hungry. They lose touch with their natural body rhythms of hunger and satisfaction due to dieting, bingeing or compulsive eating cycles. If you learn to listen, really tune in and feel your body, you will find that your body will tell you when you need fuel and it's time to eat. Children naturally have this ability of knowing when they are hungry and want to eat, and refuse food when they don't want to eat because they're not hungry. Dieting and compulsive overeating suppresses your natural ability to know when to feed yourself. The following exercises allow you to start recovering that natural ability. So now, explore the idea of letting yourself get hungry before you eat and tune into the feeling.

Relearning how to feel

When is the last time that you allowed yourself to feel hunger? Perhaps you would be willing to try this experiment. Instead of just putting food into your body when you're not hungry because you think you may feel hungry later, allow yourself to experience actual body hunger. This may be anxiety-provoking, but you can lessen that anxiety by reassuring yourself that you can eat anytime you want to. you're just experimenting with your feelings. As you're getting accustomed to this style of eating, carry some of your favorite foods with you wherever you go to decrease your anxiety regarding hunger.

If you're feeling a familiar feeling that you usually feed to make go away, check in with your stomach and see if it's really hunger. If you think that it isn't, then don't eat. Figure out what the feeling is. It could be nervousness over an upcoming presentation, or something else that really can't be fixed by food.

If it is real stomach hunger, see how strong it is. Sometimes you're hungry only for a little something, and sometimes you are thirsty. If you know you are feeling actual body hunger, then go ahead and eat whatever will satisfy that hunger. While eating, notice how the food tastes and feels in your mouth. Be aware of how the food feels in your stomach when you eat it, and your level of satisfaction. As you eat, continue to notice how it is feeling in your body. Also, let yourself feel the satisfaction of feeding yourself. Check in with your body and see if this is really the food for which you are hungry. If not, reevaluate your hunger or the choice of food, or both, but if it is not delicious to you, don't continue to eat it. Eat only the best, most satisfying, finest food you can get.

Learn to pay attention while you're putting food into your body. Are you stuffing the food into your body without really tasting it because of feelings of shame or guilt? Take your time and notice what's going on with you when you're eating. Make every time you eat an exercise in expanding your awareness about your relation-ship to food and your body. You're worth that kind of effort, aren't you?

Don't indulge in preventative eating. That's when you eat a little (or a lot) extra now, because you might get hungry later. That's the old diet mentality, the idea that you can never get enough of what you love and crave, so you had better load up now. Let go of that old idea. Live for the moment! Eat just enough to satisfy your-self now. Remember, you can have more later if you want. From what you learned in previous tips, make sure you have your favorite foods around you, so you can feel safe without stuffing yourself.

Don't eat when you're not hungry in order to please someone or "make nice". If you catch yourself eating when you're not hungry, be aware that you're eating for a reason other than hunger.

Using this process of feeling how hungry you are and eating just enough to fill that hunger will help you know how much food you actually need to feel satisfied. It will start to make you more aware of the many times that you eat for reasons other than hunger. Knowing this, you can make a choice whether or not you feel like accepting that second dinner at Aunt Sophie's because you're hungry or just trying to be nice.

The Hunger Scale

Here is a tool that you may find valuable in becoming more aware of just how much you need to eat. You can use this imaginary hunger scale for gauging your hunger and satisfaction levels. Then you can eat only as much food you need and be a lot more comfortable in your body.

- **Level One**, you feel empty; you haven't eaten for hours, and there's definitely a strong, physical hunger. You're really out of fuel, and need to feed yourself. You may even feel a little lightheaded. If you've eaten a light dinner the night before, this could be your hunger level before breakfast.
- **Level Two** is when you are quite hungry, and could eat a good meal. Food is important at this level, and your thoughts about food and desire to eat are strong.
- **Level Three** would be the feeling that you could eat something, and it's easy to think of a food that would be tasty.
- **Level Four** is feeling just a little hungry, as you would an hour after eating a good meal. Food is not uppermost in your mind.
- **Level Five** is basically feeling satisfied. You don't feel

hungry and you don't feel full. You experience satisfaction and that "just-right" feeling. You feel perfect with regard to your stomach. It's quite easy not to think of food at level five.

- **Level Six** is having eaten a little more that your body needs. You're not really uncomfortable, but you've satisfied your body hunger and you're slightly past the point of really wanting to eat. If you were paying attention, you would feel quite full if you stopped eating now.

- **Level Seven** means you are eating a lot more than you need. If you stopped here, you wouldn't have to eat again for several hours. You may have allowed yourself to get too hungry before eating, and have eaten too fast, so you can't tell yet how full you are. You are either unaware of the discomfort, or need this level of fullness to feel safe.

- **Level Eight** is when you begin to feel quite uncomfortable. You know you've gone way past what you need to eat to feel full, and there are other reasons that you're still putting food in your mouth.

- **Level Nine** feels as if you'll never stop eating and you hate yourself for doing this. This level is painful and brings about intense self-loathing and recrimination about your body and your relationship to food.

- **Level Ten** is your worst holiday nightmare. You feel bloated, guilty and ashamed. You know you'll have a bad food hangover from a binge such as this. You promise yourself you'll never eat this much again and resolve once again to get control of yourself and your eating.

Many of us don't know how much food it actually takes to feel satisfied. This scale is used as a tool for you to help notice how hungry you are, and eat an appropriate amount. I recommend that you let yourself reach a level three before eating, and then keep assessing your feelings of fullness until you're at five or six. When you go to seven or beyond, you know that you're eating for reasons other than hunger.

Of course, everyone overeats at times, because we've let ourselves become overly hungry, or simply because the food tastes really good. However, we're not talking about stuffing yourself occasionally at a party or on Thanksgiving. It's what you do daily that is important here. If you consistently eat twenty percent beyond what your body needs to feel satisfied, you will carry around an additional twenty percent of weight. When you stop feeding yourself more than you need to feel satisfied, the extra weight will simply start to drop away, without any feelings of deprivation or effort at restricting your intake.

The Eating Guidelines

The eating guidelines can change you life. (Notice that they are not called "rules". Why? So you will not feel rebellious, and use them only if they make sense to you.) Eating in accord with these guidelines will challenge many of the ideas that you have regarding eating. However, using them can dramatically change your relationship to food, and your body will change accordingly.

1. Eat when you feel hungry. Ask yourself, am I hungry for food, or something else?

2. Eat only what you want, and exactly what you want.

3. Eat until you are no longer hungry. Your definition of fullness may change over time.

4. Sit down and eat in a calm environment.

5. Be aware of how the food tastes, feels, and affects your body. Pay attention many times as you eat to how full you feel.

6. Eat without distractions such as radio, television, books, mail, newspapers, or during intense or provocative conversation. Don't eat in your car.

7. Do not change your food choices in the presence of others. Eat whatever you want to eat around anyone. This is very important. Don't apologize about or explain your food choices. If someone insists that you should be eating "diet food", say, "This is what I feel like eating, please don't be judgmental." If that doesn't satisfy them, say, "Why are you so interested in what I'm eating?"

8. Enjoy the experience and focus on your pleasure.

You're not a diet victim

One of the benefits of feeding yourself on demand is that you learn that it is possible to be satisfied regarding food and your body. You are the one who controls your eating. Your eating does not control you. Feeding yourself on demand allows you to get in touch with the old, ingrained habits and thought patterns that may, without your conscious knowledge, be governing your actions regarding food.

Realistically speaking, if you're isolated at a job site, or if it's the middle of the night, you won't always be able to feed yourself exactly the thing that you want. Do the best you can. You can become very resourceful in giving yourself what will satisfy you. The result of this kind of self-care and self-nurturing is that you begin to feel that your needs and desires are important. You're important enough to pay attention to your needs and to care for yourself.

Because the idea of dieting and deprivation is not an option for you anymore, you must look for ways to make feeding yourself "on-demand" work. Learn to find ways to care for yourself and to overcome feeling like a victim of your circumstances. You're not a victim! Shift your thinking from being someone who's trapped in unsatisfactory circumstances, to that of being one who's very resourceful in taking care of oneself. You are learning a different way of caring for yourself. Know that you're worth it. The extra planning and effort will pay off in the realization that you can take care of yourself in the way you most prefer, that you don't need to rely on anyone else to tell you how, and that you think highly enough of yourself to do it. Doesn't that realization feel good?

Homeplay

1. Dining Experience

This week make time for at least one true "dining experience." Choose a time when you can really treat yourself well, set a beautiful table, eat exactly what you want, without distractions, in harmonious surroundings. Slow down and enjoy your meal with appreciation and gusto. Use the Hunger Scale above. Rate your feeling of fullness from 1-10.

2. Love Letter

Imagine for a moment that you are someone else – an imaginary close friend who loves you completely and unconditionally. Write a letter that explains all the reasons behind your feelings. Why does this person love you so much? Why did this person choose you for a friend? Use the following format, where all you need to do is fill in the blanks, or create your own.

Dear _____ (Fill in your name)

Do you know how much I love you? I think you do. But do you know why I love you so dearly? Let me tell you.

I love you because: _____

And also because: _____

The first time I met you I knew I wanted to be your friend because:

Just being with you makes me feel:

You don't have to... _____

_____

Because you already... _____

_____

I admire you in so many ways. Here are a few of the ways I love and admire you: _____

_____

Every now and then you act a little... _____

But it's OK with me because I know... _____

_____

I would be afraid to be this frank with most people, but not with you because: _____

Your loving friend and best fan,

(Sign your name here)_____

This Week:

Eat when you are hungry

Eat whatever you want to eat

Eat until you are satisfied

If you overeat this week, notice your thoughts and feelings about it and write them down here:

Why did you overeat?

What messages do you give yourself either while you're eating or after.

What was going on for you before you overate?

If you feel angry about eating, can you be gentle and forgiving with yourself?

TIP 7

LEARN POSITIVE SELF TALK, DIET FROM NEGATIVITY

If one could really get what one wants by being hard enough on oneself, everybody would have everything that they want. However, you may have noticed that beating yourself up hasn't achieved the results you have hoped for regarding weight loss or your ideal body.

You probably hear things like, "Fat people just eat too much; just eat less and exercise more; the hardest exercise is pushing away from the table." We've all heard these statements a hundred times. If following them worked for you, then you'd be where you want to be. But they haven't helped. However, to one degree or another, you've agreed with them, at least subconsciously. The self-contempt that you have for your body, your eating habits and your weight stems, to a large extent, from messages that you've heard, believed, and made your own.

We all have voices inside our heads that are constantly giving us messages about all kinds of things throughout the day, including our looks, what we're wearing, how we do things, how people are relating to us. And, especially if we feel that our body is not right, we talk to ourselves about our size and what we're doing about it. We're constantly judging and criticizing ourselves for being the way we are, but we hardly ever praise ourselves.

Notice how judgmental you are of yourself and your appearance the next time you look in a mirror. Having a bad hair day? See a new wrinkle or a blemish? Do you tell yourself how awful these things are? The truth is that these thoughts are not doing you any good. In fact, they are doing you a great deal of harm. You don't realize how powerful these negative messages are, but you end up feeling bad about yourself because of them. The negative thoughts and messages that you give yourself throughout the day contribute to the lack of self-esteem that you feel and decrease your ability to go after and get the things you really want in life. Self-judgment and negative self-talk keeps you feeling like a victim.

Notice when you have thoughts like, "I'm so fat." Or, "Nobody my size ever goes skating on the boardwalk, people will laugh at me." Or "They aren't hiring people like me." This kind of thinking breeds unhappiness and fosters resentment, which creates negative feelings that must then be suppressed, often with food. Telling yourself how awful you look pollutes your mind like toxic waste.

It's not your fault

There was a time when you naturally and spontaneously accepted the body you have. Although you started out innocent, at some point you looked in the mirror and said, "I don't look like I should. My body is not acceptable to me. I am not right." Where did these thoughts and ideas about yourself come from? You didn't come up with these ideas on your own. There were outside stimuli that gave you the idea that your body wasn't okay. Being a member of a family, or a group, or society, you are conditioned by forces outside yourself which shape your values and ideals. It's not your fault, but you are at the affect of these ideals. Your dissatisfaction with your body size or shape came from messages you received from family, society, and the media about how you should be.

Some ideas come from our families. If someone whose opinion is important to you has been critical of you in the past for being overweight, you "internalize" his or her way of thinking and accept it as your own. "Well," you think, "if Mommy thinks I'm too fat, then I guess I am." You are innocent and impressionable. Then some part of you also adopts the idea that you're too fat.

Some ideas come from the media. When you see only images of slender women as being loveable and desirable, then you naturally surmise that to be desirable, you must be slender. you're constantly being told that thin is better and that eating is somehow awful and shameful, especially for fat people.

But even though you're constantly getting these messages, know that the messages are not your ideas; they were learned. You can assert that you do not accept that the body styles that we see on television and in magazines are the only appropriate way to be. You can achieve YOUR ideal body, although it may not be a reed-thin model's body. Love yourself the way you are, and this will help you to get thinner, no matter what your genetic size and shape. Believe in and assert a viewpoint more appropriate for you. Is it really so necessary for everyone to conform to one very specific idea of how all bodies should be? Become the best YOU can be by starting today to accept yourself the way you are. By not making your current size wrong, you will feel less anxiety and subsequently eat less.

Look at some of the awful ways that you treat yourself for being overweight. Realize that beating yourself up about the way you look does nothing to help you. This abuse harms your self-esteem. You have told yourself that if you're tough and you discipline your-self enough, then the latest fad diet will work for you. But it doesn't make sense to expect to achieve a positive outcome by forcing yourself to diet because you see yourself as wrong the way you are. By making yourself and your body wrong, you just feel worse. In the long run, using negativity to motivate yourself never works.

You deserve to eat, just like anyone

Have you ever noticed feeling ashamed of your appetite and desire to eat? Do you feel that people are judging you regarding your body size and your food choices? There is a very pervasive sense in our society that you are not allowed to eat if your body size exceeds the popular ideal. Start to become aware of these thoughts and feelings when you are eating in the presence of others, in a social situation or even at the checkout counter at the market. Rebel against accepting these ideas! The shame you feel about eating was a learned response. You didn't suddenly dislike yourself because of your size. At some point you accepted the input of others who, for reasons of their own, felt that your size wasn't acceptable.

In our society, there is no denying that people tend to judge you based on your size. But you needn't allow this to dictate the way you feel about yourself and your food choices. Allowing yourself to be dictated to is an extension of your desire to please others with your personal appearance. Assert to yourself and others that you deserve to be whoever you are, exactly as you are right now. To counter these feelings that you don't deserve to eat, tell yourself continually that you are a worthwhile human being, no matter what your size. After all, if you were to lose weight, you would be the same person. You would still have the same idiosyncrasies and quirks that you have at your present size. Doesn't it make sense that you also have the same strengths and wonderful qualities? You won't be any more fun, loving, smarter or savvy when you lose weight – you'll just be thinner. Recognize that you have the same qualities right now that you would have if you were to lose weight, and start appreciating yourself now!

By doing this, you can start to live your life based on your strengths. When you feel a desire to make a change, that is a decision for self-improvement, and you will be more motivated to do whatever it takes. You're motivated from a place of feeling okay the way you are, not the feeling that you must change to be okay with society. You're making a change because it's the next thing you feel like tackling, like mastering a martial art, or learning pottery. Your self-esteem doesn't need to be dependent on your size, and you can think of changing your body as an interesting challenge.

Get rid of your scale

The next step in eliminating negative self-talk is to get rid of one of the worst perpetrators of negativity – your bathroom scale. The purpose of this is to help you remove the obsessive focus on your body size, based on a number. The scale keeps you focused on a number as a measure of your self-esteem – another aspect of the diet mentality. "150 pounds is better that 160 pounds, 110 is better than 112," and so forth. Where does it end? When will you be thin enough to finally be good enough? I can tell you from experience, the answer is never.

If losing is good, then gaining is bad, and this mindset wreaks havoc on your self-esteem. If one week you're a good person based on what you ate, are you a bad person if you ate differently and gained weight the next week? The point is that we don't think, "Oh, I'm a little heavier this week, because I've been eating more." We tend to take it personally and extend the idea that we're a diet failure into every aspect of our lives. We demoralize ourselves completely because of one issue – we haven't been eating in align-ment with our body goals.

So if you've ever experienced five pounds of metal and glass ruining your entire day, you're allowing this inanimate, mechanical object to dictate how you feel about yourself, based on the number you read. You may wake up in the morning feeling light, lean and good about yourself, and then you step on the scale and discover, to your horror, that you're actually two pounds heavier. You feel defeated and depressed after you started your day feeling great. We all fluctuate two or three pounds daily depending on such things as water retention, hormonal cycles and how much food you ate or how full your intestinal tract is. So to allow the scale to dictate how you will feel about yourself is giving up your power to this object. You're giving the scale the power to make you have a good or bad day, based on a number that naturally fluctuates anyway.

Some people tell me that they're afraid that if they don't make daily weigh-ins, they'll just continue to gain weight and be completely out of control. They think that a constant reminder of not reaching their goal is a good motivator. In the long run, the scale itself doesn't help you achieve your goals. Quite the contrary, on a day-to-day basis, it serves to make you more miserable, because it's a constant reminder of what you have not yet achieved.

Be a friend to yourself

Take back control of how you feel about yourself! Decide that you're not going to make yourself unhappy, and start to wean yourself off daily weigh-ins. You will know when you start losing weight by the way your clothes and body look and feel. It's best if you can stop weighing yourself entirely. What difference does it make if you weigh 160 or 163, if you are unhappy at either weight?

As you learn the tools and start putting them into practice, your body will begin to change. Your focus will not be so obsessive about your weight, and it is common to drop five or ten pounds and not even realize it. Of course, something will be changing about your eating habits and your relationship to food, and you will be quite aware of that.

If you must diet, diet from negative self-talk

Think about the kind of boss for whom you are most motivated to do a good job – one who makes unpleasant remarks, speaks ill of you, berates you for doing a bad job and causes you stress by telling you how wrong you are? Or one who approaches you with under-standing, appreciation and compassion, and lets you know that you are doing well? If you've ever had someone in your life who has been on your back about doing something, you know that the more they nagged you, the less you cared about changing your behavior. It seems that inherent in the human psyche is a mechanism that makes us feel rebellious toward even the discipline we try to give ourselves. Maybe it's a carryover from childhood, but if you're constantly beating yourself up and telling yourself that you're bad, and that you MUST NOT EAT, there's an equally strong force in you which resists being told what to do. It's the part of you that says, "I'll show you. I won't let you change, no matter what." This habit of berating yourself doesn't promote change or self-love, and as a result, makes it harder for you to achieve your ideal body.

A very powerful aspect of this process is to be aware of the voice inside your head telling you that you're not okay the way you are. Pay attention to what you are telling yourself on a daily basis. You might be surprised. Would you say those things to anyone?

Start changing those negative messages to positive ones. This is very important. Recognize that those negative statements harm you. When you hear that little voice inside your head admonishing you, be compassionate with yourself regarding that statement. For example, you might hear yourself say, "You know that was bad for you. Why can't you control yourself more?" Or, as you're getting dressed, and look in the mirror and your internal voice may say, "I look disgusting, just look at my stomach. I hate my body!" If you catch yourself starting to say these negative statements, stop and say, "Whoa! That may have been so in the past, and that might be what I used to think, but I'm not going to get down on myself for that today. This is the first day of loving myself thin, and "loving" is the operational word. Things are going to be different for me now." The whole point is to be aware of the negative statements that you say about yourself, set them aside, and affirm the positive. How do you do that? Read on.

Change comes from a place of positivity

Many people believe that being hard on ourselves makes us reach our goals. Think about some of the mean things that you've done to yourself in the past when dieting. Have you ever put a picture of yourself at your heaviest on the refrigerator door, thinking that if you get disgusted enough, you'll stop overeating? Have you ever worn clothes that are uncomfortable and too tight, with the idea that it will serve as a reminder to not eat as much? Have you refused to go out and buy new clothes in a larger size that actually fit, because you didn't want to accept the fact that you had gained weight? Pause for a moment and reflect on how all these methods have worked for you.

Creating change from a place of positivity

It is very difficult to achieve a positive outcome from a negative standpoint. The more unacceptable that you feel you are, the less able you are to make positive changes in your life, because you feel powerless. The more that you accept and acknowledge yourself and affirm that you're already okay the way you are, the more able you will be to create lasting changes in your life. The better you feel about yourself, the easier it is to make positive changes. Slowly and surely, you will replace abusive self-talk with powerful and positive thoughts of self-love and support.

Don't expect to arrive instantly at a place of total self-love and acceptance, because the habitual negative messages you have been giving yourself are powerful and pervasive. Just remember that simply awareness can change the habit. Gently coach yourself into a more accepting attitude. Shift the focus of the self-messages from, "I hate my body, I hate the way I look, I think I'm ugly," to "Okay, this is my body now. I accept that maybe my body is not perfect, or even how I think it should look, but I'm finding new ways to care for my body. I'm moving to a place of greater love and acceptance, and doing things to feel better about my body." You don't have to say that you think your body is perfect the way that it is, or even say you absolutely love your body, although that's wonderful if you can. It's good enough for you to change the message from one of "I hate myself," to "I'm okay, this is where my body is now and I'm nurturing myself and working toward changing myself." This doesn't mean being totally unrealistic, but when you find yourself looking in the mirror and thinking negative thoughts, just stop yourself. Say, "Stop that. I like my chest and I like my face, and I'm not so happy with the way my legs look right now, but I'm willing to make a change. I'm working on feeding myself and taking care of myself." When you are able to, go further and tell yourself, "I'm happy that I have this body, it's served me well. I like this or that about myself, I'm really okay." Later on, give yourself wonderful, loving and positive messages such as, "I love everything about my body, I'm a beautiful person from head to toe, I look great, I'm so lucky to have this wonderful, healthy body."

You create a very powerful sense of well-being when you affirm the positive and nurture yourself. If you can encourage yourself, ease up on the negative self-talk, and empower yourself in the ways that you're eating and living, you're in a stronger position to improve your life and your body. The more you can relax and accept yourself being okay exactly the way you are, the less you will have to use food to suppress your uncomfortable emotions about disliking yourself. The more you accept yourself as you are now, the easier it is to change. The self-hatred that you feel for your body took a lot of negative conditioning to build up and won't disappear in a few days. Every time you catch yourself in negative self-talk, turn it around and affirm the positive about that specific thought. Create a positive statement that is the opposite of the statement you just made about yourself. Try it on for size and see if you can accept it. If you can't accept the positive statement, use a neutral one such as "I'm okay."

Self-Acceptance versus Resignation

You may worry that accepting yourself the way you are right now will lead to "giving up", or resigning yourself to being over-weight forever. "If I accept myself as I am now, what will be my motivation to change?" you ask. Past experiences of giving up may have left you with feelings of helplessness and despair. Thus, your experience with self-acceptance was based on a negative context, that of resigning yourself that certain things are beyond your control. You were left with no hope and no tools for change, plus self-loathing. And that was the end of your excursion into self-improvement.

When you give up, you think, "This is just the way it is, and it will never be any different." Resignation is a form of despair that the future will be the same as the past. The reason this type of thinking is so painful and damaging is the idea that you must change to be okay.

But what if you could change your thinking? What if you could think of yourself as okay the way you are, even though you may not have your perfect body? Then making changes becomes an adventure and a challenge, based on your desires for yourself, and what's important to you.

Believing you're okay as you are and desiring to change represents a shift of context regarding how you relate to yourself. You could think of self-acceptance as simply recognizing the reality of what's happening right now, without judgment. That is, you have the body you do, and certain things have contributed to that. It's not right or wrong; it's just the way it happens to be. That doesn't mean it must be that way forever. By simply acknowledging the way your body is right now, you can remove much of the shame and disappointment in yourself.

Start to relate to yourself here and now. Don't compare yourself to how you were in the past, or how you think you should be. Focus on your strengths and positive qualities. Think of yourself as being in a process of change, freeing yourself from old beliefs and ideas that never served you in the first place. Giving yourself this freedom prevents you from feeling stuck in helplessness. Even though you may not yet be seeing outward manifestations of weight loss, you are changing from the inside out. The first change is being positive about yourself.

Every day is an opportunity to make choices that will either carry you further toward your goal, or help you to learn something about yourself. As long as you are engaged in the process of learning what makes you tick, clarifying your values, and becoming healthier emotionally, it could never be seen as simply "giving up." As we've noted, if negativity were a good motivator, the most negative people would be the most successful. Face your challenges with a positive approach, and expect things to work out for your benefit. See how this new outlook helps change your attitude about your body. Know that your body has served you, and begin to love yourself based on that fact. That knowledge will help you to have more confidence in your ability to achieve your ideal body.

HOMEPLAY

1. Tuning in to your internal voice

This exercise will help you examine the internal and habitual messages you give yourself. Read the message, and then write down any contradictory message you hear in your head in response to this message. Repeat each statement until you have no more contradictory statements to write down next to each one. Pay attention to your emotions and body responses as you do this exercise.

For example, read, "I (your name), can say 'no' to (someone significant in your life) without losing his/her love." You may notice that your first thought after you state this is, "But I know I'll feel guilty," or some such similar thought. So you write this down. Then you repeat the statement to yourself: "I (your name), can say 'no' to (for example, my mother) without losing her love." Then you may hear your mind say, "But she'll be upset with me..." Continue saying the statements to yourself and writing down your thoughts until your mind runs out of responses.

Say the statement:

I_____, can say no to _____ without losing his/her love.

Write out your mind's response:

_____

Say the statement:

I_____ , deserve to be my ideal weight.

Write out your mind's response:

_____

Say the statement:

I_____ , deserve love in my life.

Write out your mind's response:

_____

Say the statement:

I_____ , am totally worthy to have what I want in my life.

Write out your mind's response:

_____

Say the statement:

I_____ , am just fine as I am.

Write out your mind's response:

_____

Say the statement:

I_____ , deserve to succeed at whatever I do in life.

Write out your mind's response:

_____

Make up some statements of your own about those things that are important to you.

2. Alternatives for dealing with pain

This week, whenever you find yourself wanting to eat as a result of emotional pain, distress, anxiety, anger, depression, loneliness or other non-hunger reason, stop and ask yourself whether eating will remove the pain or make you feel better. Look for an alternative way to nurture yourself. Vivation is the most effective tool you can use to resolve your negative feelings, so learning how to Vive is your first choice in dealing with emotional pain. However, you can use the list below instead of eating. Or write one of your own and carry the list with you. Whenever you find yourself reaching for food as comfort, pull out the list. Try at least one alternative, and then decide if you still want to eat.

Organizing, getting rid of clutter, and cleaning out your office or living space always feels good and gives you a feeling of getting light, lean and streamlined.

- Clean out your desk, answer correspondence
- Clean house, vacuum, laundry, clean windows
- Organize closets, give away discards
- Make gift lists, start Christmas shopping early
- Set up a budget
- Update your resume
- Organize income tax paperwork for this year's return
- Balance your checkbook
- Create a scrapbook
- Look through and organize photo albums
- Buy a new address book and transfer numbers

Do all the errands you've been putting off – put gas in the car, have duplicate keys made, take care of shoe repair, dry cleaners, post office, alterations, have the oil changed in your car.

- Get the car washed or wash and polish it yourself
- Look in the classified ads for a new income opportunity

Exercise clears the cobwebs out of your head, and the endorphins that are released during physical activity will help you feel better immediately and reduce stress for hours afterward.

- Go for a hike in the hills and enjoy the scenery
- Take a walk
- Play with dog, take dog for a walk, teach old dog new tricks
- Ride your bike on errands
- Practice yoga
- Roller skate
- Go dancing
- Create opportunities for simple social activities
- Call someone on the phone
- Rent a movie and invite a friend over to watch
- Snuggle with someone you love
- Visit a friend or family member
- Go out to a movie
- Write a letter to someone with whom you haven't communicated in a while
- Go shopping or to the mall
- Meet new people through the Internet
- Organize a group to go out dancing, bowling or to a nightclub
- Ask a friend to join you for a trip to the swap meet
- Borrow a kid and play
- Give yourself alone time for puttering around the house and taking care of yourself.
- Read a book or magazine
- Do deep breathing or visualizations
- Meditate or take a nap
- Write in your journal or write a story or song
- Make a list of all the things you have to be grateful for
- Say or write affirmations
- Get a pedicure

- Schedule a massage, ask for or trade a massage
- Give yourself a massage
- Play music or dance
- Scream into a pillow, cry or beat a pillow
- Give the dog a bath
- Water and care for plants
- Go to the gym
- Get a facial or give yourself one
- Pluck eyebrows
- If you are upset with someone, resolve the conflict
- Pray
- Do CCB (see Chapter 9) while you soak in a jacuzzi
- Listen to subliminal tapes
- Play solitaire
- Drink water
- Write a love letter to yourself
- Try a new hairstyle
- Make a "wish list" collage – perfect figure, great trips, romance
- Go to a hobby store and find an interesting project
- Start an art project or finish an ongoing one, such as crocheting an afghan or painting a still life
- Start a major project such as furniture painting
- Buy wallpaper stencils and paint and apply to room
- Just get out of the house for a while
- Go to the park
- Go to a toy store
- Go to a card shop – buy and send cards just for fun
- Go to a book store and browse
- Go to a travel agency and get brochures on dream vacations

- Drive to the beach
- Go to the zoo
- Go the library or a museum

Reaching out to others is a way of getting out of your own preoccupation. Connect to your love and compassion for others by volunteering your time and energy to those who are less fortunate than you. Being with and helping heal those who have serious problems helps you to put your problems in perspective. Service heals pain.

- Volunteer to spend time with elders or helping out at a shelter for battered women or the homeless
- Visit an animal shelter or pet store and give the animals love and attention

3. Deep Breathing/Ideal Self Imaging

At least two or three times over the next week take the time to sit down and do the following deep breathing/ideal self imaging exercise. If you feel ambitious, make a recording of the questions with pauses after each, so you can really concentrate on your inner experience as you do this exercise.

Take some deep breaths, relaxing as you exhale. Imagine how you would look if you had your ideal body. Visualize how your hair looks, and your face. Look down and see how your body looks and how you are dressed. Notice every curve and proportion of each area of your body. Spend a few minutes looking at the various parts of yourself, getting a clear picture of your ideal body.

Imagine yourself in different situations with your ideal body, looking really great. Your hair is wonderful, your clothes are just right and your body is just the way you want it to be. Imagine yourself in a family situation, seeing members of your family and your friends. How are they responding to you and you to them? Include your mother, father, siblings, old boyfriends or girlfriends, and anybody who may have been unkind to you in the past.

Do you feel good in the presence of others, happy and proud of yourself? Do you feel diminished in any way? Or, conversely, are you feeling arrogant or superior, better than the others? Are you incurring the jealousy of anyone? What are people saying to you? How do you feel?

Change the setting and see yourself with your ideal body at work. How are your co-workers responding to you? What kind of comments are you receiving? How does this feel to you?

Imagine yourself in an intimate situation, with a lover or spouse. How are they responding to you and you to them? Does this feel comfortable or threatening?

Spend some time examining what life will be like as your ideal self. What are you feeling? How are people responding? How can you make it more OK for your ideal self to exist?

This Week:

Eat when you are hungry

Eat whatever you want to eat

Eat until you are satisfied

If you overeat this week, notice your thoughts and feelings about it and write them down here:

Why did you overeat?

What messages did you give yourself either while you were eating or after?

What was going on for you before you overate?

Even with other emotions present, can you be gentle and forgiving with yourself?

TIP 8

HOW YOUR EXCESS WEIGHT SERVES YOU

Getting in touch with how your weight and food pre-occu-pation serves you brings an interesting awareness to the situation. Eating works as a wonderful coping mechanism. It is a way to combat boredom and reward yourself. Food can also alleviate anxiety, or keep the harsh world away. Because so many people can relate to food, talking with friends about the latest diets and your struggle with your weight can create a wonderful bonding atmo-sphere. This doesn't make food and eating wrong, and it doesn't make you wrong to use food to relieve stress or for other reasons. But now that you are ready to make changes in your life and eating habits, it is beneficial to acknowledge that sometimes you use food. Some people use alcohol or drugs. They are all means of coping; some are more destructive than others.

Taking responsibility for all of your choices, in every area of your life, means that you can now applaud yourself for your desire to find other, healthier ways of coping than using food to solve life's problems.

When fat's the way you want it...

You may not want to acknowledge this, but sometimes you keep on extra pounds because there is a benefit for you. We may all have different reasons, but there may be reasons that you choose to hold on to your weight. Staying fat may actually have a "payoff" and work better for you. If you find yourself reacting against this idea, just try to stay open-minded about and notice if any of the following situations ring true for you.

- You've been overweight for a long time, and may have received much negative attention from your family and friends for it. With negative attention often better than no attention at all, perhaps you've kept on weight for fear of losing the attention that you *do* get.

- Your parents or spouse are constantly telling you to lose weight. Staying heavy may be your statement that you won't be told what to do, even if it might benefit you. Is your weight the symbol of a power struggle between you and someone else, a "screw you" to someone who wants to make you change? It may be a tangible, visible statement of "I'm going to be however I want to be, no matter what you say."

- You may have fears about making changes, or desire to avoid exchanging unknown problems for the ones that are familiar.

- If you have your ideal body, would you create disapproval from friends or relatives? Are you keeping extra weight on because you're afraid of making people jealous, or having other people think you're "stuck-up?"

- If you had your ideal body, do you think you would be unbearably arrogant?

- Were you rewarded with food as a child, or were you a fussy eater? Did your parents encourage you to eat and praise you when you did? We have all heard of the starving children in China, or wherever our parents said to get us to clean our plates. Did your parents reward you for being captain of the Clean Plate Club?

- Do you continue to be "good" to please your parents, when being good no longer has any bearing on your relationship with them?

- If you only dream about being your ideal size and never

experience the reality of it, you can indulge in unfounded fantasies about how your life would be if you were your ideal weight. By never finding out what life would be like, you can allow yourself these fantasies, which are probably better than reality would be. In addition, no matter how close we get to our ideal body, we continue upping the ante on our ideal life fantasy.

- Your sense of yourself as a powerful person is connected to your large size. You may fear of losing that sense of power. You feel more important when you are able to "throw some weight around." Some people fear being thin, weak, fragile, vulnerable, or "thin-skinned." Being thinner allows them to feel the slings and arrows of the world too intensely. Keeping extra weight on may actually make sense if you felt this about yourself, wouldn't it? So someone who feels this way can stay sturdy and strong.

- In the arena of relationships and sex, there are many possible reasons to stay fat. For example, if you don't have confidence in your ability to say "no" to unwanted advances, staying fat is a good way to avoid the issue entirely. Extra weight is also used as a barrier to avert attention, to attempt to make yourself unattractive or invisible, or to add an extra layer of insulation against unwanted glances or remarks. If this resonates with you, think about whether your strategy works. After all, there are many big beautiful women who attract attention. Does the extra weight really achieve your purpose? Doesn't it make more sense to heal the feelings related to being seen and appreciated, than to try to hide behind a wall of weight?

To help you understand this more, here are additional reasons to contemplate why being fat may work better than being thin.

- If you were to think of yourself as sexy and desirable, you may fear being promiscuous. Keeping the extra weight on can be a form of self-punishment or guilt from having had an affair. If you have a jealous mate, and fear confronting that issue, extra weight can be a means of guaranteeing that you won't be "too attractive" to others.

- Another thought regarding relationships – everyone wants to be loved, but sometimes we fear we are loved and wanted for the wrong reasons. What better way to test a partner's love than to keep on extra pounds and make sure he/she loves you for your "real self?"

- You might have a fear of success, a fear of being too visible in your career and getting too much attention. If you don't have the self-esteem to accept compliments graciously, the extra weight may serve to keep compliments away. Many times I've had women tell me that after dieting, they heard others remark how great they looked. Not being able to accept the appreciation of others or feeling too exposed, they slowly and surely gained back all the weight they'd lost. Then they hate themselves, not recognizing that the weight served to protect them from emotional situations with which they weren't comfortable.

- As odd as it may seem, some people have the fear that they will not have anything to occupy their time, or problems to solve. They may be reluctant to give up the struggle with their bodies and weight, for fear it will leave a vacuum in their lives, and nothing to deal with. These last two ideas are subconscious, of course, but still operate as dynamics in keeping on extra weight.

When confronted with all of the issues that food helps to avoid, it's easy to see how we might want to avoid the being smaller. We may prefer to keep the problems we have rather than exchanging them for "new" problems. "At least they're MY problems, and I know what to expect," this thinking goes.

EXERCISE

Here's an exercise to help you understand why you may be carrying extra weight. If you feel that you don't need to do this part, ask yourself if it's because you feel like avoiding thinking about the issue. Instead, be open to gaining beneficial insights regarding your relationship to your body and weight. Take the plunge; tackle the exercise and confront the feelings.

Write down your responses to the following questions and statements. Write as much or as little as you like, and be as honest with yourself as you can. Write your responses quickly, without intellectual censoring, and then go back and review your responses more thoughtfully. Be open to surprising yourself with your answers.

1. One of the things that compulsive overeating helps me avoid is:

_____

2. Another thing that compulsive overeating helps me avoid is:

_____

3. Some fears I have about giving up overeating and/or losing weight are:

_____

_____

_____

4. Some of the fears that I have about being my ideal weight are:

_____

_____

5. Do you feel that extra weight protects you from unwanted sexual encounters?

_____

6. Did you ever gain weight because of uncomfortable or painful circumstances in your life?

_____

Taking your life off hold

There are many ways in which we put our lives on hold because of our current size. An interesting belief system that operates for people who are overweight, or have a negative body image even at normal weight, is that once we get our ideal body, our lives will begin. We keep our lives on hold and never do the activities we love. We don't go after what would bring us real satisfaction, because we feel our body isn't right. This allows us to live in the realm of fantasy, without ever making the effort to achieve our dreams. "My life hasn't started yet, because I'm fat," the thinking goes, "but as soon as I'm thin, my life will be really good, I'll have the relationship I want and I'll be more successful in my career, I'll get the part I want, or run the marathon."

You make your current life wrong and blame it on the fact that you're overweight. You avoid doing the sports you love because you think people will be looking at and judging you because of your size. Or you avoid getting into an intimate relationship because the thought of having to bare your body scares you.

You avoid these things because you're uncomfortable with yourself and feel shame about your body and eating. You don't have a way to deal with the feelings that these experiences bring up. You feel that your life would change if only you could change your body.

Think for a moment about the things you avoid because you feel that your size or shape isn't right. What have you put off until you finally lose twenty pounds? Wouldn't it be a shame to go through life never having the relationship that you want because you believe that you need to lose five pounds before you are able to think of yourself as desirable and available? A woman once told me that even though she is normal weight, if she is in a room with women thinner than herself, she absolutely believes no man would be attracted to her. Do you resonate with that kind of thinking?

The unfortunate mindset that this creates is that dieting is the answer to all of your problems. This kind of thinking is a way to avoid unhappiness with your life and emotional issues that you don't want to confront. So you blame it on your weight and believe that dieting is the means to change that. But you know that dieting doesn't work. Even if you do manage to lose weight, your emotional issues are still there. You may feel them even more strongly when you're thinner. So you probably gain the weight back and get lost in the vicious cycle – blame your weight, diet, lose weight, feel unstable, gain weight, feel like a failure, hate yourself, blame the weight, and so on.

The way out

In Tip 7, we looked at the idea of accepting yourself the way you are right now, as a means to becoming the person you want to be. What if you were to feel that you could have the life you want as you are now? Start looking at what you want in your life and find ways of creating that at your present weight. Yes, right now! Why not? If today you feel too shy to go after and get a companion or lover, you'll still feel shy when you are thin. A thinner body will not make shyness go away. What solves shyness? Practice in being around people, learning social skills, and increasing self-confidence. How does food or eating resolve shyness? It doesn't. Shyness is one of the emotions that can't be solved by food. See Tip 9 on how to use Vivation to resolve the emotions that keep you from having the relationship you want, and then go after it.

For example, people tell me, "Oh, no man/woman would be

interested in me at the weight I am now." That's simply not true. Anyone can have fulfilling and exciting relationships if they believe they can. Look around and you'll see that many larger people have friends, lovers, husbands and wives. You need to change the way YOU think and feel about yourself, and people will start to perceive you differently. When you start loving and appreciating yourself more for your unique beauty, talents and strength, you'll be surprised at how differently others relate to you. They'll start finding things to appreciate about you that they never noticed before, simply because you project a different self-image. Your new self-confidence says, "Yes, I AM an exceptional person, a treasure trove of uniqueness, including love, humor, compassion and strength. I value myself as a complete human being."

As you begin to value yourself as a whole person with all your unique resources, qualities and idiosyncrasies, you will feel attractive, whatever your weight. If you value these things in yourself, your self-esteem will rise. When your self-esteem rises, you will love yourself at any weight. Perhaps you will strengthen your motivation to reach your ideal weight. Or perhaps your excess weight will matter less. When you love and value yourself, your weight will not be an impediment to a relationship or having anything else you want in life.

Stop blaming your weight for your not doing what you love or going after what you want! If you lack motivation or perseverance to learn a new sport at your present weight, what will change if you were to lose weight? The emotions will still be there at your smaller size, so why not just go after what you want right now? Life will always bring large and small challenges. Take steps to start tackling the challenges you can handle now and go on to the larger ones later.

Dreaming

Sit back and relax for a moment and think about what you would do or what you would do differently if weight were not an issue. What kinds of things would you want to do in your life, even if you could never change your body size?

- Would you join a social club, go square dancing or bungee-jumping?
- In what activities would you like to participate if you were your ideal weight?
- What else might change for you, and how?
- What are some things you dream about and wish for?
- If you were your ideal weight, would you actually go after these things?

Objectification equals Dehumanization

YOU are not your body; your body is a part of you. Many people have come to view their bodies as ornamental, rather than as the instruments through which they act, feel and live. Both women and men can feel that their value as people comes from having attractive bodies. They think that if their body doesn't fit well into our cultural aesthetic, which is arbitrary and changing, they lose value as an individual.

Observe people on the streets. How many of them fit into the current fashion of being tall and extremely thin for women and/or broad-shouldered and narrow-waisted for men? Yet all of these people are essentially valuable and unique as individuals. They are all potentially loving and lovable to someone. It is a marketing and advertising triumph that we all want to look like fashion models in a genetically varied world.

Why are we so obsessed about body types? What is wrong with having a variety of body shapes and sizes? Our culture conditions us to view ourselves in constant comparison to others. Susan Kano, author of *Making Peace with Food*, states, "It is only through extensive and continual conditioning that an intelligent human being comes to see herself as an ornament, whose first priority is the attainment of a slender body, rather than as a complete human being who has a myriad of other concerns and unlimited potential." Isn't this a powerful statement? It reminds us how much we focus on having a perfect body instead of on having a balanced existence. There are so many ways in which life can be fulfilling; stop using weight and body size as a measure of value, both for yourself and others.

Beauty is not only what society defines it to be. Figure out ways of valuing yourself for who you are, based on your resources and strengths. Feeling good about yourself comes from the inside. You create feeling beautiful by learning to believe you are beautiful.

Ultimately, no matter how perfect you make your appearance, if your self-esteem is based on your looks, the simple inevitability of aging will eventually undermine you. Seek out and emulate women who could be role models for you, who have made a contribution to the world other than simply looking good.

Begin to notice and reject in thought, word and action the destructive social prescription to be as thin as possible. Replace "fatism" with respect for people regardless of size. Notice the times when you make snap decisions about people because of their size, and remind yourself that everyone has wonderful and not-so-wonderful qualities, just like you do. Your judgments are as rough on yourself as they are on other people, so try to be easier and gentler in your thinking.

Notice how your judgmental or competitive thoughts isolate you from others. Broaden your ability to appreciate and see the beauty in all those around you, including yourself, regardless of size. Start to think of your body, independent on your weight, as both a trusted friend and a treasured home for you to enjoy and use fully, rather than as an object to be admired or judged.

EXERCISE

Objectifying yourself and others

Write down your thoughts and feelings in response to the following questions.

Do you objectify others? That is, do you judge people based on their appearance alone?

How much do you judge yourself on the basis of your appearance?

Do you respect fat people less than thin people?

If so, does this seem fair and ethical?

Do you remember an occasion when you were initially critical of someone and later really like him or her, because you found them wonderful and interesting?

What helped you get past your first impression?

Notice the thoughts you have when you are around people at a mall or restaurant.

Are you constantly evaluating, judging and comparing?

Do you say things about others that you wouldn't want said about yourself?

How does objectifying others affect you? Does objectifying others lead to judging yourself based only on your appearance?

Do you believe you would be a better person or have more determination to achieve your goals if you were thinner? Why or why not?

Does your behavior change depending on your weight? If so, how?

Make a list of what you like about yourself and your recent accomplishments that have nothing to do with your appearance.

HOMEPLAY

You already know the disadvantages of being overweight and having constant problems with food and eating. What may be less obvious are the benefits you get out of having this problem.

1. What are the benefits of fat/weight and having an issue with food?

Consider issues such as getting attention from a doting parent who is constantly concerned about your well-being and always after you to lose weight; or keeping away the opposite sex because you don't feel that you can handle someone's advances.

What are your payoffs? Write down all the ways in which fat and food issues have served you, the purpose or value of them in your life, and the good reasons you have for not giving these up.

Example: Weight or issues with food may:

- Serve to keep people who aren't interested in the "real" you away.
- Allow you to avoid relationships that you think may be scary or painful.
- Keep you from confronting more serious issues that you don't want to deal with.
- Keep you from confronting your fear of success or failure.
- Serve as your excuse for not doing/having what you want.
- Provide you with a sense of security, safety and power.

Some of the things that my struggling with my weight may help me avoid are:

2. From resentment to self-assertion

Being overweight, we often put others' desires before ours and then resent doing so (or them). To lessen feelings of resentment when you feel others are making overwhelming demands on you, begin to notice if you put others' needs or demands before your own.

This week, whenever you have a problem with someone requesting your time or resources, take the following steps. First, clarify the problem. For example, if your boss/child/spouse wants something done right away and you feel you do not have the desire or time, ask if they will discuss it for a moment. Determine exactly what they need and whether it must be done today and by you. Explain your problem with meeting their request and propose an alternate solution. For example, perhaps someone else might handle the task, or you might do it tomorrow. Perhaps you could rearrange the priorities of your tasks. If the problem is urgent and you are the only one who can do the particular task, perhaps someone else could do one of the other things you were going to do. Define the problem, review the options and find a solution that works for both of you. When solving problems, it takes practice and willingness to learn to consistently take our needs as well as others' into account. Honor your feelings and let it be known that your desires are as important as anyone else's.

3. Relaxing in the face of fear

When you have thoughts about your body that make you uncomfortable and create anxiety, stop to take a moment and review that thought. For example, you may be planning on going to a class reunion or a wedding, and you think, "I'm fat, and I'm afraid of so-and-so or my family seeing me like this." Then you crash diet, which may have worked for you in the past. But now you know that is not really an option, since it keeps you on the diet merry-go-round, losing and then regaining more than you'd lost.

Don't attempt to push the fear away. Denial only serves to make the fear stronger. Acknowledge that you feel this way. Tell yourself, "I feel uncomfortable seeing _____ when I'm at my present weight." Acknowledge that your body is the way it is right now, and that your body MAY not change in the next few days or weeks. Nurture yourself by saying, "Okay, this is how my body is, I am not going to be 10 pounds thinner by tomorrow. Panic and worry are not going to be of any use in changing that. So I choose to accept myself as I am."

Assume the positive. Know that you are working toward healing yourself and this may take a little time. You can't be any better in the moment than you are. Accept that you're in a process of change for the better, and that's good enough. Let go of the fear, acknowledge where you are, and the positive direction in which you are focused with your food/weight issue. Focus on your strengths. Change will take time and self-acceptance is part of the process.

4. Imagining your ideal self

Sit down in a quiet place and do some deep breathing to help you relax your mind.

(If you're feeling ambitious and really want to create a powerful process, a tape is a good tool to make for yourself. Just be sure to leave pauses in the dialogue to give yourself time to create the mental picture.)

Picture your ideal self in your mind's eye, complete with the perfect hairstyle, makeup, and outfit. Imagine yourself in different situations as your ideal self, exactly as you would look and act if you had the body, looks, hair, face, and clothes you wish for. Examine what life will be like as your ideal self. This can be a really powerful exercise, so don't rush through it. Going slowly will allow you to get the full benefit.

In your visualization, pay close attention to your experience. Examine your feelings and write down your responses to how people are responding to you as your ideal self in the following situations:

- Career – co-workers, boss, colleagues
- Social – peers, friends
- Family – mother, father, siblings, relatives

- Relationships – sexual, non-sexual
- Dreams – doing the things you wish for yourself

What are the ways in which you can make it more comfortable for your ideal self to exist?

This Week:

Eat when you are hungry

Eat whatever you want to eat

Eat until you are satisfied

If you overeat this week, notice your thoughts and feelings about it and write them down.

Why did you overeat?

What messages do you give yourself either while you're eating or after?

What was going on for you before you overate?

Can you be gentle and forgiving with yourself?

TIP 9

GET RID OF EMOTIONAL BAGGAGE

Relate to your feelings differently

Until now, we have been talking about our feelings and how they can affect our behavior regarding food. I'd like to now give you a couple of powerful tools to use in your healing process. These tools will help you address and resolve the negative emotional issues that are often the cause of compulsive eating.

Conscious Connected Breathing works very well to heal the underlying emotions that are very often the cause of overeating and overweight, or negative body image at any weight. Conscious Connected Breathing (CCB) begins to bring up the suppressed emotions that you have been using food to stuff down. If you are now willing to feel some of the feelings that you have been eating to avoid, you can rapidly move beyond the need to eat to get away from, well, basically, yourself. As you love and accept yourself more, you will not need to eat for any reason other than hunger, and you will eat an amount appropriate to your hunger, and lose weight in a completely natural and organic way. You'll be feeding yourself that which you really hunger for, and finding yourself to be satisfied on less actual food.

To do Conscious Connected Breathing, you simply breathe in a way where there are no pauses in your breathing…as soon as you take a deep inhale, you begin a relaxed exhale, and then start the next inhale, and so on. Make sure that you fill your lungs completely on the inhale (take in as much air as you can), and then just let go of your breathing muscles, and let the exhale flow out.

Do at least 15 minutes of this kind of breathing every day. You can do it in the bathtub or lying down, or when you take a break at work. Pick a place where you can pay attention to what you're feeling as you're doing the breathing, and just let yourself feel whatever comes up.

Another much more powerful tool to use for healing suppressed emotions is Vivation®. http://www.vivationusa.com

Vivation is a self-development technique that works at the feelings level to resolve negativity in all areas of your life. Vivation includes methods you already use to some extent to deal with negative emotions and resolve them. By learning and using this technique, you will gain mastery at resolving negativity, and transform your life into a great adventure. You will heal your uncomfortable suppressed feelings at a cellular level, allowing the energy that it took to keep those feelings suppressed to return to you for your creative use. Situations that upset you in the past will no longer upset you or govern your behavior in the present. Your relationships will improve, you will experience better health, and more enjoyment in life.

As compulsive overeaters, we often feel we would be in a better position to control our weight if we could control our feelings. By learning the Vivation process, you will no longer need to control your feelings or emotions, because you will learn to experience your emotions in a very different way, a way that adds to your overall sense of well-being, rather than detracting from it. You can learn to turn obstacles into opportunities and take the lemons that life gives you and make lemonade. You can relate to your feelings in such a different way that they no longer bother you or cause you to act in ways that might be working against you.

By learning how to change your relationship to your feelings, you can create what we call "integration" of the feeling. That is, you will learn to shift how you relate to that feeling from a negative context to a positive context. (For our purposes, we are using the word "context" to mean "how you look at something," "point of view," or "attitude"). Integration is the realization that a feeling you previously held as negative or bad can be beneficial and/or pleasurable. By being able to integrate your emotions, you learn how to eliminate internal conflicts and become happier and more powerful. You learn that there are always unlimited choices about how you relate to a situation, when previously you thought that there was only one way to think about it. Knowing that you can choose puts you in a position to do something about the situation. Rather than feeling helpless and victimized, you recognize that you are the one who creates how you will relate to what you experience in life, and that, in every case, is empowering.

Content and Context

Every experience has a physical part and an emotional part. The physical part is the event or situation itself, what is happening in the moment, and we call that the "content." For example, your being the middle child is the content of your birth order, a basic fact. The emotional part of being the middle child is the way you feel about it, good or bad. We call this part the "context."

A negative context is any experience in which you are comparing the reality of a situation to an imaginary standard and deciding that what you're imagining is better that what you are experiencing. The situation is something that in fact, could be either good or bad depending on how you look at it, but you are choosing to look at it in a way that makes it seem bad. In other words, when you hold something in a negative context, you are "making it wrong," which causes you to have certain feelings or reactions in your body. You feel your thoughts in your body, and the way you feel about something affects your thoughts.

On the other hand, when you cease making anything about your situation wrong, you are experiencing life in a positive context. A positive context is one in which you accept what is actually happening, rather than comparing it to the way you wish it would be or some other imaginary standard. Other imaginary standards would be, the way it used to be, the way you wish it would be, or the way it is for someone else. Experiencing life in a positive context, you can be happy with life exactly the way it is. In the Vivation process, you learn how to shift your relationship to the experience you are having, so you can enjoy that experience more, or have it make a contribution to you in some way.

Vivation is not primarily a mental process. Although you are using thought to create a positive context, the shift occurs at the body level. Vivation is not pasting positive thoughts over negative beliefs; you are actually shifting how you relate to your experience. This will change your experience in your body from one of unpleasantness to one of pleasure.

Some examples of positive contexts are:

- Extending unconditional love to all parts of yourself, especially to those feelings you haven't liked in the past
- Being grateful that the experience is not worse
- Enjoy being on the threshold of change
- Noticing that what you are experiencing is funny
- Being grateful you have all the emotional components of a fully functioning human being

You can shift your context at a kinesthetic (feelings) level as well without creating any context other than openness. By simply embracing the feeling and paying attention to it, you will resolve the negativity and the feeling that is there will integrate into pleasure.

Your context for your body

How do you feel about your body? At your present weight, perhaps you're making yourself wrong for not being thinner. Holding your present weight in a positive context, you could be grateful that you're as thin as you are. But if you are comparing yourself to an imaginary standard of how thin you think you should be, you're holding your body in a negative context and making yourself wrong. This creates uncomfortable feelings. When we feel negative toward ourselves, we often resist the feelings, and do anything we can to not feel them. This starts a downward cycle of negativity from which we try to escape by eating.

When you use the Vivation process, you learn to acknowledge, accept and even to enjoy the feelings in your body that you have formerly tried to escape from or avoid. You shift the way you feel about something or the way you think about it to a positive context, and you experience that feeling as pleasurable and enjoyable. This shift causes you to no longer resist the feelings that are there, so you no longer need to suppress them with food or any other substance. This is what we call "integration," the ability to have all your feelings and emotions contribute to your well-being.

Making lemonade from life's lemons

To understand this more, remember an experience you didn't enjoy at the time, but now can look back on and realize was a good thing. For example, many people have had the experience of breaking up with their first sweetheart. Although painful at the time, in hindsight you realize it was for your benefit. Be grateful for the relationships you've had since then, and realize that they wouldn't have happened if you hadn't broken up with your first sweetheart. Learning to relate to an initially painful experience with gratitude changes the feelings in your body and allows you to feel good about yourself. This is what we call integration.

Can you think of any other experience you've had that you didn't enjoy at the time but can look back on and know that it was for the best? Developing your ability to integrate allows you to reduce the time between an experience and your recognition of it as beneficial. If you can relate to the experience, which initially seems unpleasant as beneficial, you can feel good about it. Even if it was a horrible experience, you can be grateful you had the strength to survive it. This creates the shift from a negative context to a positive context. Holding something in a positive context is not positive thinking about a horrible circumstance. Rather it allows you to heal the inner pain at a very deep level by appreciating your strengths.

You choose your experience

To further illustrate the idea that you can choose to change the way you perceive something, here's an example: Do you know that how you think about the proverbial half-filled glass of water affects your happiness? Is the glass half-empty or half-full? If you perceive it as being half-empty, you can bemoan the fact that you don't have more water, wonder what you did to deserve so little water, and so on. This causes you to have feelings of limitation and suffering. On the other hand, you could choose to celebrate the half-full glass of water, be grateful about it, think about how lucky you are, and celebrate water-drinkers everywhere. It's completely up to you. The glass of water does not change, but the feelings in your body do – you are deeply affected by how you think about it. By choosing to look at the situation in a certain way, you create uncomfortable feelings in your body that you must deal with somehow. Compulsive eating is one of the least successful ways to cope with those feelings. Whenever you are unhappy with your present circumstances, in every instance, it is because you are comparing your life is to an imaginary standard of how you think life should be.

How to shift your experience to a positive context

You can learn to be your own best friend and cheerleader. That means you lovingly accept every aspect of yourself for the purpose of creating the body you want from a place of positivity. We have already noted that whenever you make yourself wrong, you have unpleasant feelings in your body that beg to be suppressed by eating. This leads to a downward spiral of frustration, self-loathing, more eating, and so on. So it is very beneficial to develop a technique of making yourself right by learning to shift your relationship to the feelings in your body.

Vivation Technique

Vivation is a powerful process that includes circular or connected breathing, focused awareness of your feelings and conscious relaxation to make you happier and more powerful. You will learn to love yourself the way you are, and use that self-acceptance as a stepping-stone for positive change.

You can get the CD set at http://www.vivationusa.com

If you do not have the CD set, read on and you will learn that it is possible to create similar benefits by learning to shift your context mentally. You will be able to experience exactly the same changes in your body whether creating integration intellectually or kinesthetically, by embracing the feelings and opening up to them in an honest and loving way.

Using tools you already know

The Five Elements of Vivation

We all have the ability to "Vive" to some extent already. You are breathing right now. That is using the first element. Some degree of relaxation is always possible. That is the second element. The third element is awareness of the feelings in your body. If you can feel gravity, you are already experiencing a feeling. We all enjoy some of our emotions, from laughter to fear, as many people enjoy seeing scary movies and riding roller coasters. This is the fourth element. At the same time, you are also doing the fifth element (exhibiting your willingness to create a beneficial outcome) because you are reading this information. So you will be learning how to use skills you already have to create more happiness and peace of mind with Vivation.

When doing Vivation, we use all of the elements simultaneously. Rather than thinking of these as steps, we can think of Vivation as one process, made up of five components.

The Five Elements make up an acronym: BRAID. Let's start with the fifth element, because if you understand this element, the others will be easier to use.

The Fifth Element

DO WHATEVER YOU DO, WILLINGNESS IS ENOUGH

The Vivation process always works because we have a natural willingness to improve the quality of our lives. This element takes all of the difficulty out of doing Vivation, because you don't have to use all the elements perfectly to have the process work for you. There is no need to worry if you're doing everything right, because your willingness to resolve negativity is enough to make the process work perfectly every time. Willingness is really the only essential factor to succeeding with Vivation.

The First Element

CIRCULAR or CONNECTED BREATHING

Most people inhale, exhale, and pause in between. In Vivation, we connect the inhale to the exhale so there are no pauses in between. The emphasis is on the inhale, and the exhale is always relaxed, no matter how fast or slow you are breathing.

Breathing in this specific pattern allows the suppressed feelings in your body to gently be uncovered and healed. By itself, breathing does not cause integration, but helps you to gain a better rapport with your feelings in order to give them the love and attention they need for healing.

Circular breathing has three criteria:

1. Your inhale is connected to your exhale, with no pauses in between.

2. Your exhale is completely relaxed and not controlled at all.

3. You breathe in and out either through the nose, or in and out through the mouth. Either is good. Whichever feels best to you is best.

You can learn to vary the speed and depth of the breathing to "fine tune" the feelings and control the intensity of your experience. If your experience is too intense, breathe slower or shallower, or both. If you want to experience more intensity, breathe faster and fuller. To integrate sleepiness or unconsciousness, use fuller and faster circular breathing. To integrate either physical or emotional pain, use fast and shallow breathing. To maximize pleasurable feelings, use slow and full circular breathing.

Faster breathing gives you more awareness of the overall pleasure of aliveness. Slower breathing gives you more awareness of the specific patterns of energy in your body. Fuller breathing is used to intensify the experience, and shallower breathing is used to make the experience more subtle. You can maximize your good feelings by using fuller and slower circular breathing. Play with the speed and depth of your breathing to find the best rapport with the feelings in your body.

The Second Element

COMPLETE RELAXATION

Relax all parts of your body that are not used in the breathing, and completely relax on each exhale. The more you relax, the more you are able to notice which area of your body is asking for attention. Then focus on that feeling. This element also includes relaxing in the presence of the feeling. By doing this, you learn that feelings and emotions are simply patterns of energy in your body, which are always flowing. You will often find that by simply relaxing in its presence, the feeling changes.

The Third Element
AWARENESS IN DETAIL

If you were to go to a concert, you would open up your hearing awareness in order to enjoy it more. To use this element, open up your feeling awareness and pay attention to the feelings and sensations in your body. Your body sensations are direct and immediate. When I talk about feelings, I mean physical sensations, emotions and patterns of energy in your body. Focus on the sensations themselves. Feel gravity to begin. Also, you don't need to label them to feel them; many feelings are combinations of emotions.

This element also serves to bring you into the present, and allow you to see that your feelings change from moment to moment. Questions to ask yourself regarding the sensations in your body are: Where am I feeling this the strongest? How large an area does the feeling cover? Is it dull or sharp? Is it stronger on the inhale or the exhale? What color is the feeling? Does the feeling have a texture? Allow yourself to become aware of all the sensations and focus on the most prominent feeling in your body. Even if you don't think you are feeling anything, that feels a certain way. Don't try to create feelings, just notice what is there.

The Fourth Element
INTEGRATION INTO ECSTASY

You don't need to do anything in order to be happy. When we hold our experience in a negative context, we make ourselves unhappy. Using this element, you can learn to accept or enjoy your feelings as they are, empowering yourself to use all of your emotions to your advantage. By finding a different way to relate to your feelings, you change them. When you shift your point of view about your experience to a positive context, that shift creates pleasurable feelings in your body. The fourth element is the emotional skill of consciously choosing a positive context, rather than holding on to a negative one. Integration is resolving the difference between the way we imagine a situation should be and the way it is.

EXERCISE: *Learning to shift to a positive context*

1. Make a list of ten things about your body, your relationship to food, or something else in your life that you don't like or wish you could change. Notice that when you contemplate the ten things on your list, you get certain feelings in your body that you would probably prefer not to feel, or at the very least, don't enjoy. Let yourself feel them and don't eat.

2. Compare the things on your list with the list below, "How to Shift Anything to a Positive Context." Start with the first thing on your list and compare it with the first thing on this list. Think about the item on your list in the positive context of the list below, and see if thinking about it differently changes the way you feel about it. Your feelings will either change or stay the same. If they do change, you'll be able to feel the energy shift in your body. If the feelings change, fine, there's one more thing to be happy about and enjoy in your life. If the feelings don't change, go on to the next thing on the Positive Context list and think about your item in relation to the next positive context. You are engaging in the process of learning to change your relationship to your feelings using your intellect.

If it does shift to being more positive, (or integrate), then go on to both the next thing on your list and the next thing on the Positive Context list and do it again. If the feeling does not integrate, stay with your same item and continue applying a different positive context to it until it shifts. The way you will know that it integrates is by paying attention to your feelings. If you continue to have an unpleasant feeling, it means that you are still making the thing on your list wrong. If you are able to shift the context and integrate the negativity, you will feel better when you think about that aspect of your life.

For the purpose of this process, you should consider it an integration if you feel your energy move in the direction of feeling good about something you formerly felt bad about. Your feelings about something can still be a little bit unresolved, and yet you can feel much better about them.

All you need to do is find three or four statements that work for you among all of the ones below, and you will be well on your way to making a quantum leap in enjoying more of your life.

How to Shift Anything to a Positive Context *(Excerpted from Vivation: The Science of Enjoying All of Your LIfe, by Jim Leonard)*

1. Find a way to enjoy it.

2. Notice that what you are experiencing is not infinitely bad. Be grateful that it's as good as it is.

3. Expand your gratitude for your existence to include the particulars of what you are experiencing now.

4. Surrender to the fact that your life is the way it is whether you resist it or not.

5. Just decide to accept it.

6. Cultivate a sense of fascination with it. Let it engage your natural feelings of curiosity.

7. Expand your compassion to include all people who experience similar things.

8. Expand your compassion to yourself for struggling with this as long as you have.

9. Think about someone or a pet you love deeply and send that same love to the feeling inside you.

10. Be open to this feeling making a contribution to you somehow.

11. Extend unconditional love to all parts of your experience, including what you're feeling right now.

12. Be grateful you are strong enough to have survived your past.

13. Enjoy the newness of the feeling; or, take comfort in the familiarity.

14. Appreciate that it is exactly the way it is for only one moment in all of eternity. Enjoy it quickly before it integrates.

15. Notice your nearness to your goal, rather than your distance, and take responsibility for achieving your goal.

16. Appreciate that it helps you get to know yourself better.

17. Acknowledge that it would be okay to lighten up about it.

18. Imagine what it would be like for it to be exactly as it is but for you to feel okay about it.

19. Notice the extent to which you already do feel okay about it.

20. Just decide to make peace with it now.

21. Enthusiastically exaggerate your feeling to the point of absurdity.

22. Enjoy the intensity of the experience.

23. Be comfortable with its familiarity.

24. Be grateful for your ability to feel.

25. Be grateful the right thing is activated.

26. Know that by feeling it you are healing it.

27. Honor it as a teacher.

28. Stay open-minded about it.

29. Notice how it strengthens your character.

30. Notice how it strengthens your determination.

31. Be grateful for what a good story this will make later on.

32. Even though it doesn't seem pleasurable, open up to it as though it were pleasurable.

33. Feel the tingle of aliveness within the pattern of energy in your body.

34. Trust that you are strong enough to handle this.

35. Realize that it's not as bad as your worst thoughts about it.

36. Praise yourself unconditionally.

37. Be grateful that it's in your past.

38. Just give love to the part of you that's activated.

39. Be very gentle, patient and caring with yourself in the presence of the feelings.

40. Let the pleasurable feelings of strength and vigor that are already present in your body help you to integrate this.

41. Experience every sensation as white light or healing energy.

42. Let go of any desire to control the circumstance and surrender to the moment.

43. Appreciate the unique beauty of the feeling.

44. Be grateful this experience lets you know you're alive.

45. Be grateful you have such marvelous excuses for your negativity.

46. Trust your body.

47. Trust that everything is evolving perfectly.

48. Welcome the challenge.

49. Surrender to the fact that you can't win a war against your own feelings.

50. Enjoy this because it's the only life you've actually got.

The Three Points to Remember

In addition to learning to shift the way you relate to the feelings, it is helpful to remember the following points while doing Vivation:

1. **Explore the subtle details within the feeling itself.** Focus your awareness on the feelings closely enough so that you can feel when they change. All feelings change from moment to moment, and it is helpful for you to feel that there is a flow to the energy in your body.

2. **Inhale through the feeling.** Notice where the feelings are in your body. Focus on and inhale through the strongest feeling, as if that part of you was suddenly permeable to air. Feelings can be emotions, physical sensations or patterns of energy. Use circular or connected breathing. Breathe comfortably so that the inhale is connected to the exhale, and there are no pauses in between. Relax on the exhale, rather than blowing it out. Let it <u>flow</u> out.

3. **Enjoy the feeling as much as you can.** If your experience isn't infinitely agonizing, (and I doubt that it is), there is always even a small amount of pleasure available to you in any experience. And especially if there is only a tiny amount of enjoyment available in the experience of the moment, it is important that you make the effort to connect with that pleasure. Not all experiences will be enjoyable in the same way, but what matters is that you attempt to wring every drop of pleasure from whatever experience you are having.

You can use the Vivation CD set, available from Benesserra Publishing at http://vivationusa.com/pages_top-nav/products_services.htm, to practice this powerful healing technique on your own. Vivation is taught internationally by Vivation professionals in private sessions, group classes and seminars.

For further reading about the Vivation process, read *The Skill of Happiness: Creating Daily Ecstasy with Vivation* by Jim Leonard, available at http://www.amazon.com. Also good are *Vivation: The Skill of Happiness,* by Jim Leonard and Phil Laut, *and Your Fondest Dream: The Power of Creativity,* by Jim Leonard.

HOMEPLAY

Every day this week, choose and use one of the Positive Context statements that will enable you to shift the context about whatever you're feeling. Use that statement throughout the day to integrate negativity as it arises.

To illustrate, if you have chosen the statement, "I'm open to this feeling contributing to me in some way," you could use that to gain insight about why you are having those feelings, and further, to allow that curiosity to help you feel better about the feelings. For example, if you have had an abusive past, you could concentrate on the feeling of strength you have used as an inner resource that helped you to survive your past. Gain benefit from this resource, which has helped you survive as well as you have, because things could always be worse. The experience could also lead you to have compassion for those who experienced the same thing, and thereby have more compassion for yourself. In this way, you consciously turn feelings that detract from your sense of well-being into feelings of enjoyment.

Another example. Let's say you have a zillion things on your "to-do" list, and you feel frantic about getting everything done. You could bounce off the walls or you could take five minutes, sit down in a quiet place, connect your breathing, relax your muscles and say to yourself, "In what way can I be grateful for my life?" There are probably as many ways to feel good about your life as there are things on the to-do list, such as being grateful you have something to do, or that you're a conscientious person who makes an effort to get their tasks done. You could experience your enthusiasm about getting them done completely and on time. These thoughts will give you pleasure, instead of discomfort that more isn't getting done in the same time. Focusing on your nearness to your goal is always more helpful in getting to where you want to be in life, rather than focusing on the distance.

So every day this week, choose a different "integrative" idea. When you notice an uncomfortable feeling, use the connected style of breathing you learned earlier. Relax, become more aware of the feelings in your body, say some of the Positive Context statements to yourself and see what happens. Be open to the feelings changing. If they don't, that's all right, simply acknowledge the feelings and continue practicing relating to them in a positive way. Just relaxing about the fact you are feeling them can change them, too. Most importantly, remember it's your willingness to improve the quality of your life that makes positive change happen.

Affirmations

After giving yourself thousands of negative self-talk messages over the years, you need to not only become aware of these self-criticisms and their effect on you, but also to consciously change these comments. Make positive statements, rather than negative ones, become automatic. Try saying the following affirmations aloud while driving in the car, in the shower, whenever you are alone and have the opportunity, and silently to yourself at other times during the day as you learned in Tip 7, "Learning Positive Self-Talk". Or try writing them down here and noting your response.

Choose any of these affirmations that appeal to you, or create your own. Use at least three over the next week.

I, _____, accept my body as it is; it has served me well. Now I am willing to let go of excess weight.

Your mind's response:

_____

_____

I,_____, love my body and myself unconditionally.

Your mind's response:

_____

I,_____, am learning to feed myself with things that satisfy me.

Your mind's response:

_____

I,_____, can lose weight by loving myself completely.

Your mind's response:

_____

The more I relax about my body and eating, the less important food is for me.

Your mind's response:

_____

It is easy for me,_____, to love myself.

Your mind's response:

_____

I, _____, am now eating my way to thinness.

Your mind's response:

_____

I, _____, forgive myself for eating when I was not hungry.

Your mind's response:

_____

I, _____, deserve to achieve and maintain my perfect weight, no matter what I eat.

Your mind's response:

_____

I am getting better and better every day, because I love and appreciate myself more.

Your mind's response:

_____

This Week:

Eat when you are hungry

Eat whatever you want to eat

Eat until you are satisfied

If you overeat this week, notice your thoughts and feelings about it and write them down here:

Why did you overeat?

What messages do you give yourself either while you're eating or after?

What was going on for you before you overate?

Can you be gentle and forgiving with yourself?

Remember:

ACCEPT.

    ACKNOWLEDGE.

    ALLOW.

TIP 10

PUTTING THE TIPS INTO PLAY

Honoring yourself with food

Remember that we have decided that there are no bad foods. All foods are legal, and unless they are poisonous or moldy, or you are allergic, there are also no foods you shouldn't eat. Honoring yourself with food means finding a way to eat that will increasingly contribute to your well-being, no matter what you are feeding yourself. Never tell yourself that you are bad for eating anything. In fact, eliminate telling yourself you are bad for anything unless you like to experience the feeling that results from self-abuse.

Honoring yourself with food means that you are giving yourself what you want and need to feel good about yourself. You not only find out exactly what food you need to feel satisfied, but think about how the food is going to affect you, physically and emotionally. This tip is about taking responsibility for your food choices and accepting those choices, whatever they may be. You decide if you want to eat a certain food, based on your values. Does the way you are eating support what you want for yourself? Ask yourself if the food honors the person you want to be, the person that you're on your way to becoming.

The point is, with regard to a certain food, you know you can have it, but do you really want it? Do you want the momentary satisfaction of the food in your mouth and stomach, or do you want the deeper satisfaction of knowing that you're helping yourself achieve your ideal body? Either choice is okay. You make it okay, knowing that when you're ready to make changes, they will happen spontaneously, not by forced denial or restriction. When you remove all the shame and "shoulds", what's left are your choices. This is truly taking responsibility for yourself.

You're in the process of change. You are becoming a different kind of person than you were before you had this much awareness of your food habits. You've discovered by now in what ways you have been using food to fix some kind of hunger other than physical hunger. And you also know that it's important to address the issue directly, rather than use food to try to solve the situation.

You are becoming the kind of person who deals directly with your desires rather than suppressing your emotions and using food or your body shape as a distraction. You've learned to ask, "Will eating get me what I really want, like a hug or some loving attention?" If it won't, you reconsider your actions. If food won't solve your issue in the moment, then why eat? For example, if you're angry with your mate, you may get the urge to eat chocolate. You recognize the feeling for what it is – a desire to suppress your feelings of anger and lose yourself for the moment in sensory pleasure. But you also know that, indeed, the chocolate itself won't do anything about your angry feelings. In fact, if you binge on chocolate at this point, you'll be even more upset. So you can look past the desire of the immediate moment to see that eating will not solve your problem of being upset with your mate. You need to deal directly with that situation instead of distracting yourself with food.

As you begin to realize that food won't solve your problems, you can be more selective about what, when and how much you eat. This is a process of trial and error, don't expect yourself to be perfect at it right away. You might habitually eat something that doesn't honor you. After doing that a number of times and noticing that it doesn't work for you, you may decide not to continue eating that food. Be gentle with yourself no matter what you're doing, understand that by allowing yourself to have what you want, you will naturally grow out of eating for non-hunger reasons. When food stops serving a purpose, you will eat when you are hungry, and stop when you are full. You will eat until you feel satisfied, not more, and lose weight easily and keep it off. You will honor yourself continually by the way you take care of yourself.

The basis for change –
accepting yourself as you are right now

Decide that you will accept yourself as you are now and that it's okay to be in the process of change, no matter what anyone else says. If you encounter people in your life who want to judge and evaluate you, thank them for sharing, but don't let their feelings or opinions sabotage you in your decision to love and accept yourself. Know what you are trying to accomplish, and remain steadfast in your resolve not to beat yourself up about your size.

This comes down to learning about your own values, about how you view your body, your relationship to food and what you want in life. Don't let external factors and the people around you change your feelings about what's right for you. The more you are empowered by feeling good about yourself, the stronger you become in asserting what you want and what you don't want in your life.

When you accept and honor yourself as you are now, you feel better about yourself and the easier it is to change. This doesn't mean that you lie to yourself and refuse to acknowledge any negativity. Let yourself gracefully be where you are, accepting that you're working on yourself and doing the best you can. Your gentleness and willingness are enough to create the change you're seeking.

People love to give unsolicited advice. Have courage and listen to your own counsel. Discard erroneous ideas about how you should live your life, if these old ideas aren't aligned with treating yourself with love, respect and acceptance of everything about yourself, including your body and your relationship to food.

As you shift your inner perception about yourself, regardless of your outer physical appearance, the perception of those around you will shift. Others will perceive you in a different way. They get their cue from you and how you feel about yourself. Work with your own thoughts and feelings. As you start to feel better about yourself, you will radiate a different energy. You will look different. You will start to relate to yourself differently. Work on integrating your suppressed emotions using Vivation, and the change will be dramatic.

Living in the present – swap or sweep

Do you have different wardrobes to match your different sizes? Do you have a range of sizes in your closet, from the super "skinny" clothes, to the really "fat" clothes? Are you holding on to clothes that may have fit you long ago, but don't anymore? You may have these things from when you were younger and smaller that you just can't bear to get rid of. But every time you look at them, you feel bad. They not only serve as a silent reminder that you've gained weight, but you may also feel that it would be a waste of money to throw them out.

Perhaps it's time to go through your closet and get rid of items that fit you years ago and that you've been saving for the time you can fit back into them. Give them away, or at least pack them up and put them in a box somewhere out of sight. These clothes aren't in alignment with your current body. Clothes that don't fit or look good on you right now make you feel bad and you don't need that.

Have a garage sale, a clothing swap with friends, or donate your old clothes to charity. You don't need these silent witnesses in your closet staring at you everyday, making you feel negative about the size you are now. Get them out of your life. Treat yourself to a couple of new items that fit and look great on you. Take along a good, honest friend, and purchase some clothes that make the most of your good features – a nice bust, long legs, a small waist, or your pretty face. When you wear this outfit, you'll feel like absolute dyna-mite, because this is an outfit that expresses you, not your body size.

Ending food addiction is about honoring yourself and accepting yourself where you are now. It's about feeling good in your clothes and what you're wearing, no matter what your size. Wear clothes that fit, that aren't too tight, that don't feel uncomfortable, in fabrics that feel wonderful to wear. Cleaning out your closet and living in the present gives you extra space, both in your closet and in your mind. It allows you to recognize that, "Okay, this is where I am now, this is my starting point, this is the first day of the rest of my life," and move on from there. Doesn't it make sense that if your body size happens to get smaller, you'd want to go shopping for new things than wearing the old clothes that are probably out of style?

Are you postponing life until you are the right size?

There is nothing except your own beliefs and emotions to keep you from following your dreams and going after what you want.

Make the decision that you will not allow your size to keep you from doing what you want in life. Look for role models in whatever you desire to do. You will find role models of all sizes doing absolutely everything! Look around and you'll see. There are large size actors, fashion models, comics, television producers, and fashion consultants. There are people out there living their dreams, regardless of their size. Your thoughts about any activity are the only things that keep you from doing it.

Start right now. Make a list of some of the things you want in your life. Consider the thoughts you have about getting out there and doing them. Write down some of your favorite excuses and the most logical reasons for NOT doing the things you want to do. Ask yourself if you are willing to postpone your happiness until some day that might never arrive. You will come to see that it is only your thoughts and beliefs that are keeping you from living the fuller, more satisfying life you want. Try exploring the idea of living your life on a grander scale by jumping right into those things that you find satisfying and fulfilling. Now!

About exercise

Even though I don't tell people they must exercise, I believe that being active in any way is beneficial for a healthy lifestyle. I think humans were built to move, and stagnate when sedentary. But if you've been forcing yourself to exercise out of fear of gaining weight and not enjoying the activity, you're not going to continue to exercise anyway. Also, it's not useful to approach any activity from the standpoint of how many calories you can burn. It's much more fun to do activities you enjoy, and if you get aerobic benefit, so much the better. Activities such as bowling, dancing or gardening are perfectly acceptable as exercise, too. Experiment and find something you love to do. Just do what you enjoy and have fun. Concentrate on being proficient, and improving your ability and enjoyment.

Write out responses to the following statements:

Ideas I have about exercise, i.e.: everyone looks at me and I feel self-conscious):

_____

Reasons I like to move (I love rhythm and dancing):

_____

Why I dislike movement (You get all sweaty):

_____

Excuses I have used for not exercising:

_____

Some of the physical activities I'd enjoy doing if I were my ideal weight:

_____

_____

What keeps me from doing these things at my present weight:

_____

Put it all together for the life you want

In the preceding pages, you have been presented with some very powerful ideas about how to reach and maintain your ideal weight by using food only as needed to fuel your body. You also have some good ideas about how to go after and get the things that you want in your life by increasing your self-esteem, and believing that you deserve to have what you want, no matter what your size. You've learned some very powerful ways to nurture yourself, be gentle with yourself and be your own best friend. You've discovered how destructive negative self-talk is and replaced it with compassion and understanding. You've seen where judgment has brought you and have learned to become more forgiving and accepting.

As you've gone through the homeplay and exercises, you've examined many of the real issues have caused you to keep on extra weight. They have all been a part of an ongoing learning process about what makes you tick and why you are the way you are.

Perhaps you recognize that your excess weight may have served you in various ways. Now you are aware that food is not the problem. You can see that it may be your underlying feelings and emotions that need to be addressed, and you have some tools with which to do that.

This is a process about becoming happier and more comfortable with the unique and perfect individual that you are.

As you put these guidelines to work and lose weight, be on guard about slipping back into the diet mentality. The diet mentality is that of losing a few pounds, seeing your body change and feeling good about yourself, then starting to calculate how much weight you could lose over time at this rate. It's easy to slip back into thinking you can't be okay the way you are now, and that fat is bad and thin is good. Be aware what might occur is that you lose weight, and then get to a deeper level with your issues about your body, then stop losing and plateau for a while. Your mind might try to trick you into the diet mentality again. If you don't continue to lose weight at the same pace, you make yourself wrong, and the downward spiral of self-dissatisfaction starts again. Don't get hooked on that kind of thinking again, just live your life to the fullest. Be as happy as you can be in every moment. Make an effort to be grateful that life is as good as it is.

Learning to love yourself as you are heals you permanently in every area of your being. Get on with your life in the way that makes you happy. Because who you are right now is more than enough for you to go after and get what you want. Take your life off hold. There is nothing sadder than you postponing living and loving because of an extra few pounds you think make you look ugly.

Handling your compulsive overeating doesn't mean you are automatically expected to handle everything else in your life. You might find that the grass isn't necessarily greener as a thin person. You will constantly face new challenges in life, as we all do. You will still have issues to handle. With this method, though, you have what you need to believe in yourself. You have the tools to handle what-ever arises without using food. You will develop the self-esteem to believe you deserve to have what you want. You are able to be on your own side, ask for the help you need, and pick yourself up whenever you need a boost.

I wish you the very best of luck in using the tools, guidelines and principles I have given you. I am aware that there is a lot here to assimilate and put into practice. Take the process a step at a time, constantly being gentle and loving with yourself. Remember that you can't nag or beat yourself into self-improvement, so the best strategy is always to love yourself and make changes from that posi-tive perspective.

Thanks for reading this book. We hope you have enjoyed it and derived benefit. If you are interested in taking your healthy weight program a step further, we invite you to explore the Vivation technique for resolving emotional negativity as an easy to follow audiobook. Part one explains the theory of Vivation in detail, and part two provides a guided, hour-long session which will allow you to heal the underlying emotions that cause you to use food when you're not really hungry.

Available on Amazon at http://amzn.to/1r3Mc8L for purchase as an e- or audiobook.

Other titles you might like from Benesserra Publishing are *Easy Weight Loss Yoga* and *Play Better Golf with Easy Yoga* by Patricia Bacall, both available at Amazon.com.

About the Author

Felicity Garver is also the author of Gain Health, Lose Weight, available on amazon.com. GHLW is about becoming as *healthy* as possible before you try to lose weight by tuning up your endocrine system, so that you are working *with* your body to make changes, instead of against it. The book includes an easy to understand explanation of how your body metabolizes food and foods that will enhance it, so you can indeed gain health and lose weight.

You're meant to be a winner at the weight loss game! If you have any questions, comments or suggestions, please write to us at info@benesserra.com.

18114589R00069

Printed in Great Britain
by Amazon